OHIO STATE
UNIVERSITY

Student Life
in the 1960s

OHIO STATE UNIVERSITY
Student Life in the 1960s

WILLIAM J. SHKURTI

THE
History
PRESS

Published by The History Press
Charleston, SC
www.historypress.com

First published 2020

ISBN 9781540243898

Library of Congress Control Number: 2020938435

CONTENTS

INTRODUCTION

College students who came of age in the 1960s were part of a transformation unlike any seen before or since—a hostile takeover of the popular culture. Propelled by a postwar baby boom and unprecedented prosperity, these young people enjoyed opportunities that were only dreamed of by previous generations. They were told they were the largest and best-educated generation ever. They came of age when technology made mass culture pervasive and when the barriers to exploring, experimenting and expressing themselves fell dramatically. They established a generational bond that redefined the nation's popular culture with unprecedented speed and power.

The forces driving this revolution coalesced on college campuses, where sheer numbers ensured oversized implications. Much has been written about the changes that roared through the nation in the 1960s; most of it has focused on the politics of protest, especially at the elite colleges and universities on both coasts. But profound changes also took hold among the middle-class young people in the nation's heartland. This cultural revolution occurred with surprising speed and staying power.

Very little has been published about what happened at the ground level on individual campuses, like the Ohio State University. Fortunately, Ohio State has digitized its student newspaper, the *Lantern*, and its yearbook, the *Makio*, allowing easy access for both researchers and casual readers. Together, they provide an excellent record of student life in an extraordinary era.

INTRODUCTION

This collection is designed to be a companion to *The Ohio State University in the Sixties: The Unraveling of the Old Order* (Ohio State University Press, 2016), which deals with the more substantive political and educational issues of the time. *Ohio State University: Student Life in the 1960s* covers student life outside the classroom, beginning with the 1960–61 school year and ending with the tumultuous 1969–70 year. Each chapter is subdivided into six or seven sections, in varying order:

- Traditions: The evolution of the university's social traditions, including Homecoming, Greek Week and May Week—some of which did not survive the decade.
- Party time: The creative ways students blew off steam, from toga parties to flash crowds.
- Athletics: Some of the greatest triumphs in Buckeye athletics, offset by some of the most agonizing disappointments.
- Showtime: Nationally known entertainers who came to campus, and the growing wave of youth-oriented movies playing at local theaters.
- Fashion: What students wore (or didn't) and what it said about them.
- Places: Where students liked to congregate, both on campus and off.
- Buckeye bits: Miscellaneous, exciting or unusual events.

So, hop on the fun train for a magical mystery tour through a decade when being young and in college meant you were entitled to a good time.

Author's note: The vintage photographs in this collection come from the Makio *and* Lantern *archives, where, in many cases, the original photos or negatives no longer exist. They may appear a little fuzzy or grainy compared to other photos, but they have been included because they remain the best remaining visual records of these unique events.*

1

TRADITIONS RULE

1960-61

Students entering Ohio State in the fall of 1960 found a campus steeped in wholesome traditions that fostered a sense of community in an extremely transient environment. As the decade progressed, some of these traditions were challenged and others were discarded.

TRADITIONS

The Social Big Three

The annual Homecoming, Greek Week and May Week celebrations were the foundations of the university's social calendar. By the 1960–61 school year, Homecoming had been a tradition for fifty-eight years, Greek Week for twenty-eight and May Week for fifty-five. The October Homecoming events featured float displays, the election of a queen, a parade, a bonfire and a football game followed by a dance and a concert.

Greek Week, which was held in February, celebrated the accomplishments of the 4,600 members of Ohio State's social fraternities and sororities with a fundraiser for charity, a talent show, a pop concert and parties. Although only one-fifth of the 22,000 students on the Columbus campus in 1960 were Greeks, they were all cohesive, well-organized and supported by their alumni and the university administration—and they exerted considerable influence over the social scene.

Homecoming caravan, 1960. When gas costs only thirty cents per gallon, style triumphs over fuel economy. *Courtesy of the* Makio.

Elaborately produced skits, such as this one that featured a crooning candidate for Homecoming Queen and her backup chorus, were popular ways to generate votes and enthusiasm. *Courtesy of the* Makio.

A May Week staple: a frog jumping contest. *Courtesy of the* Makio.

A highlight of May Week was May Day, which was celebrated on the first Thursday of the month with fun and games galore. Classes were canceled, and students flocked to the Oval for bicycle races, limbo contests and an auction. The day began with ROTC cadets marching in review and ended with a huge supper at French Field House, followed by a dance and concert.

PARTY TIME

Suppressed Desires and Other Themes

Homecoming and May Week were big events, but they filled only two weekends of thirty during the typical academic year. Left on their own to make plans for the open weekends, students got creative. All social functions had to be sponsored by a student organization, such as a Greek chapter or a residence hall, and they had to be approved by the university. This meant female students were required to return to their residences by curfew (usually 1:00 or 2:00 a.m. on weekends). Parties were supposed to close down at the scheduled time (usually midnight), and at least two approved chaperones had to be present to make sure the rules were followed. This, however, did not seem to limit the varieties of student-led events over the 1960–61 school year. Some of the more imaginative events included:

- Phi Kappa Tau fraternity's Beatnik Party
- Phi Delta Theta fraternity's Sweater Party
- Alpha Zeta fraternity's Peppermint Folly
- Alpha Gamma Delta sorority's Suppressed Desire Party (the chaperones must have had an interesting time with that one)
- Stadium Dorm's Untouchables/Valentine's Day Massacre Party

ATHLETICS

Frustration in Buckeye Nation

When it comes to athletics, Ohio State is first and foremost a football school. In its first ninety years, the university never celebrated a national basketball title, but a rookie coach and a group of talented young players changed all of that. In 1960, they won the national championship and emerged as one of the greatest college basketball teams ever. Unfortunately, the Dream Team's undoing the following year came at the hands of an unexpected challenger.

The 1960–61 team appeared even stronger. They stormed into March Madness undefeated—the first NCAA team to do so since 1919. Ranked no. 1 in the country, Fred Taylor's boys graced the cover of the March 21, 1961 issue of *Sports Illustrated*, which turned out to be a bad omen. After vanquishing all opponents in the NCAA tournament, Ohio State succumbed to the no. 2 Cincinnati Bearcats. Dubbed the "No-Names" after losing their star player, Oscar Robertson, the year before, the Bearcats prevailed over the Buckeyes in a stunning 70–65 upset in overtime.

Two key members of the Dream Team: (*center left*) Jerry Lucas and (*center right*) guard John Havlicek. They led a lineup of talented players who were unequaled in the history of Ohio State basketball. *Courtesy of the* Maiko,

The look on their faces says it all. The Buckeye Dream Team succumbs to the underdog Cincinnati Bearcats. *Courtesy of the* Makio.

SHOWTIME

Ride of the Decibels

In the fall of 1960, the campus area sported three movie theaters, three bowling alleys, an ice rink and a variety of other entertainment venues. But for live, big-name shows, Mershon Auditorium was the favored spot.

The high-decibel highlight of the school year came on the evening of February 14, 1961. Those fortunate enough to attend the sellout performance of the Detroit Symphony heard one of the country's biggest and best orchestras blast out "Ride of the Valkyries" from German composer Richard Wagner's *Ring* trilogy. According to *Lantern* reviewer Dee Chandler, the orchestra's climactic performance "bulged the auditorium walls." Chandler continued, "The Valkyries' wild cry, the thunder of hooves, and the clashing of the natural elements, were handled with pagan power and the full voice of the orchestra." The mesmerized crowd responded with thunderous applause.

That spring, Ohio State's theater department presented an enthusiastic production of Rodgers and Hammerstein's *Oklahoma!* It filled the Mershon stage with a cast of seventy, including thirty-four chorus members and twenty dancers. According to *Lantern* reviewer Starr Morrow, the opening performance featured "an excellent cast, sparkling ensemble numbers, exciting scenery and costumes and smooth production."

The Sweetheart of Lambda Chi

In February 1961, British actress Jill Haworth traveled through Columbus on a publicity tour for the movie *Exodus*, in which she played a Danish immigrant. When Lambda Chi Alpha member Bob Boll saw Haworth's picture in a local newspaper, he decided to throw a Hail Mary and invite her to lunch the next day with his fraternity brothers. To everyone's surprise, she accepted.

The actress looked much older than her fifteen years. *Lantern* reporter Doug Bloomfield reported that the blue-eyed blonde was greeted by "a sea of sighs" as she walked into the fraternity house. She was accompanied by her mother, Eliza Haworth, who'd canceled another engagement so that her daughter could spend time with the men of Lambda Chi. "It's nice for Jill to mix with people her own age," she opined.

"...no musical comedy to equal it... a masterpiece."   Brooks Atkinson, N.Y. Times

MAIL ORDERS BEGIN MONDAY
UNIVERSITY MUSICAL PRODUCTIONS
presents
The longest-run, most popular musical show in theatrical history.

OKLAHOMA!

Right: *Oklahoma!* was one of several high-quality musical productions offered by Ohio State's theater department in the 1960s. *Courtesy of the* Makio.

Below: Actress Jill Haworth receives a Lambda Chi sweetheart pin and a dozen roses from appreciative fraternity members. Pictured with her are (*right*) fraternity president Bruce Borchers and Bob Boll. *Courtesy of the* Lantern.

IN MERSHON AUDITORIUM
WEDNESDAY, MAY 24 thru SATURDAY, MAY 27
at 8:00 P.M.
Special Matinee, Saturday, May 27 at 2:30 p.m.

All Seats Reserved – All Seats $1.50 or University Theatre Coupon
Send Check, Money Order or Coupon to:
UNIVERSITY MUSICAL PRODUCTIONS BOX OFFICE
154 North Oval Drive, Columbus 10, Ohio
(include self-addressed, stamped envelope. Allow Two Weeks for return of tickets.)

ORDER NOW—AVOID DISAPPOINTMENT
LAST FOUR YEARS SOLD OUT

Mail Order Blanks Now Available at:

After a friendly but proper lunch, the brothers presented Haworth with a sweetheart pin and a dozen long-stemmed roses. "This is wonderful. I'll never forget Ohio now," she cooed before heading to the airport to catch a flight to Philadelphia.

FASHION

Cardigan King and the Fashion Police

Student fashion trends at the start of the decade were pretty much set by the Greeks and were largely conservative. For males, a cardigan over a white button-down shirt was the uniform of the day. While men were expected to dress appropriately, there were no written guidelines, but the same was not true for women. The Women's Self Government Association (WSGA) was the arbiter of good taste. At the start of the fall quarter in 1960, WSGA sent letters to all the deans and department heads recommending that slacks and

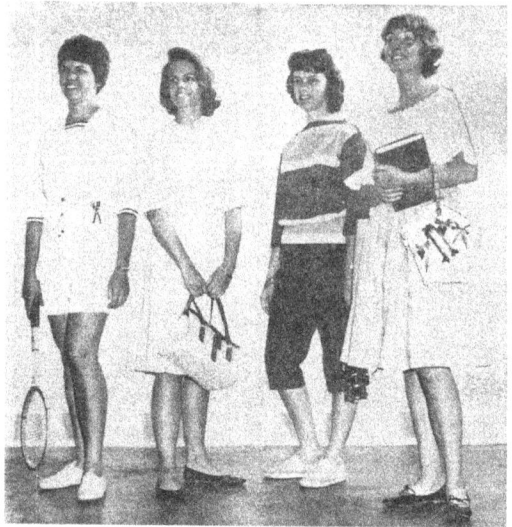

Left: Sigma Chi sophomore and Golddiggers King (the male counterpart to the Homecoming Queen) Lou Vitucci oozed cool in 1961. *Courtesy of the* Makio.

Right, from left to right: sophomore Carol Niesz, freshman Erin Malley, freshman Carol West and freshman Joyce Shur. According to WSGA guidelines, Malley and Shur are properly dressed for class, while Niesz and West are dressed only for recreation. *Courtesy of the* Lantern.

Bermuda shorts not be permitted in any class but physical education. The letters were followed with a front-page photo in the *Lantern* of four students modeling appropriate and inappropriate classroom attire.

PLACES

Drinking and Parking

When the Varsity Club opened on Lane Avenue in 1959, it deliberately catered to an older, more sedate crowd. Co-owner Larry Johnson elaborated, "We get a lot of grads and professional students and more couples than most campus bars. At least they can converse without being drowned out by loud music and shouting." Along with the Bier Stube, the Varsity Club is the only campus bar from the 1960s that is still in business today.

OPENING TODAY

THE VARSITY CLUB

Across Lane Ave. from St. Johns Arena

6% Beer Only

For All OSU Students, Faculty and Alumni over 21

Open 1 p.m. to 1 a.m.

See You Before and After the Basketball Games

Left: The Varsity Club announced its presence in this January 1959 *Lantern* advertisement. Note the reference to 6 percent beer. Under Ohio law, at the time, people over eighteen but under twenty-one years old could only drink 3.2 percent beer. *Courtesy of the* Lantern.

Below: Cars, cars, cars—too many of them for too few spaces. The problem grew worse as the decade went on. *Courtesy of the* Makio.

A different kind of place—a parking place—proved more elusive to find. At the beginning of 1960, Ralph L. Wolf, who had the unenviable title of campus traffic and safety engineer, announced that the latest round of parking changes, including the designation of A (faculty), B (staff) and C (student) zones, had "somewhat eased" the situation. As evidence of this improvement, he pointed out that "only" 8,700 parking tickets had been issued in the fall of 1959—a "marked reduction" from the previous year. In the fall of 1960, approximately 12,800 commuters visited the campus daily. So, according to Wolf's reasoning, a system in which some two-thirds of the participants violated the rules by parking illegally was an improvement.

BUCKEYE BITS

Free at Last!

This jubilant pair celebrated graduation in June 1961. Note the stylish cat-eye sunglasses. *Courtesy of the* Makio.

2

TWISTIN' THE NIGHT AWAY

1961-62

A new dance craze swept the nation in 1961, and Ohio State students took to it with enthusiasm. Swiveling their hips to the "Twist" became a popular way to destress from the grind of classes and to forget about the demoralizing football and basketball seasons. Columbus swayed to the sounds of a 1960s folk icon at Mershon Auditorium, students celebrated the tenth anniversary of the Ohio Union and madras and canvas bewitched the fashion-conscious.

PARTY TIME

Got a New Dance and It Goes Like This

Simple, provocative, fun and suggestive are some of the words reviewers used to describe Chubby Checker's wildly popular version of the dance that captured the hearts of teenagers (and, later, adults) at diverse venues, like New York City's famous Peppermint Lounge, the Kennedy White House and the Ohio State campus.

Writing in the *Lantern* during the first week of winter quarter in 1962, Marilee Sellman added her own twist to the Twist, "Pretend you're stepping on an ant while drying your back with a towel." Sellman reported that Buckeye students, who seemed blasé about the recent college fads

Left: Ohio State students twisting their troubles away. *Courtesy of the* Makio.

Below: More twisters. While one couple is really into it, some of the other dancers do not appear as enthusiastic. *Courtesy of the* Makio.

Not all parties were twist parties. *Above*: Pictured is a Baker Hall Polynesian house party; chaperones, where are you? *Left*: For those tired of twisting, a tiddlywinks contest between teams from Oxley Hall and Park Hall provides a diversion (no chaperones necessary). *Courtesy of the* Makio.

of racing beds and crowding into phone booths, embraced the Twist wholeheartedly because, as senior Tom Hathorne told her, it "swings." He added, "I think it originated as a rebellious dance to differentiate from the straight form of dancing. It's relaxing. I think more people should learn it."

Across town, Capital University president Harold L. Yochum called the dance "immoral" and banned it at university-sponsored events. But Ohio State officials were more tolerant, as the Twist swept through parties across campus. Credit for the first registered party, which took place on February 3, 1962, belonged to the men of the fourth floor of Smith Hall. Alpha Tau Omega threw the second Twist party three weeks later.

ATHLETICS

Halfbacks Galore

Buckeye Nation entered the 1961 football season with high expectations, but critics of Woody Hayes weren't convinced the coach could compete with the newer, more open offenses. They particularly disapproved of his use (or lack thereof) of halfbacks during the previous season. When Ohio State stumbled out of the gate, ending a game with the unranked Texas Christian University in a disappointing 7–7 tie, the critics howled. So, Woody flipped a switch and said, "If you want halfbacks, I got halfbacks." Sophomores Paul Warfield and Matt Snell joined fullback Bob Ferguson to provide an awesome offensive punch. The team gathered itself and never looked back, beginning a run of six straight victories.

The Buckeyes trooped into Ann Arbor on November 25 with a 6–0–1 record, and only the Wolverines stood between them and a Rose Bowl trip—or so it seemed. Ohio State dominated 50–20 before a stunned crowd of 80,444 in the Big House. The Rose Bowl invitation came as expected the following day, but there was no contract because the Big Ten and the Rose Bowl Committee had been locked in a contract dispute for two years. Therefore, under the Big Ten's rules, Ohio State's faculty council had to vote to approve the trip.

The decision may seem like it was a no-brainer, but it didn't turn out that way. Concerned by what many on the faculty believed was an excessive emphasis on athletics over academics, the council took the unprecedented

Speedy sophomore halfback Paul Warfield (*above*) and powerful fullback Bob Ferguson (*left*). Here, one would-be tackler had already been knocked down while the two remaining tacklers struggled to wrestle Ferguson to the ground. *Courtesy of the* Makio.

Sigma Nu protested the Rose Bowl decision by hanging the twenty-eight "no" voters in effigy outside the fraternity house. *Courtesy of the* Makio.

Not even talented sophomore center Gary Bradds could save the Buckeyes from another bitter defeat in the NCAA tournament at the hands of the overachieving Cincinnati Bearcats. *Courtesy of the* Makio.

step of rejecting the invitation in a 28–25 secret ballot after a tense two-hour debate. Fans were outraged. Students marched on the faculty club and the statehouse downtown in protest. Alumni sent nasty letters. Local media went berserk. Angry fans inundated university officials with phone calls and even death threats, but the decision stood.

Dream Team and the Bearcats... Not Again!

Disappointed at the turn of events, shell-shocked football fans found short-lived solace in the basketball Buckeyes, who roared into the NCAA tournament with an impressive 23–1 record. Facing the Cincinnati Bearcats in the championship final for the second year in a row, the Buckeyes lost again, 71–59.

TRADITIONS

Dogpatch OSU and Goldiggers

Worried that interest in the Homecoming Dance was waning, organizers tried to pump up the appeal by offering both a first-class band and a popular singing group on the same ticket. The dance on November 3, 1961, featured Stan Kenton's orchestra in the Ohio Union ballrooms and the popular singing group the Four Freshmen in the cafeteria—all for $4.50 a couple. Showtimes were staggered so that guests could move from one event to the other without missing a beat. Promoters hoped to sell 3,500 tickets (compared to 2,000 the year before); instead, they sold 5,500. Coupled with the traditional crowning of the Homecoming Queen, a robust float competition was held under the theme Dogpatch OSU, 1,200 mums were sold and the Buckeyes pulled out a 29–12 football victory over Iowa before 83,960 fans. Homecoming 1961 was a "rousing success," the *Lantern* declared; few disagreed.

Greek Week '62 was not as fortunate. After being burned by poor attendance the year before, Greek Week's organizers didn't book a major act, and they made everything else low key. The Greeks did manage to sell nine thousand balloons, and they raised $1,659 for the Heart Fund,

CHOKE 'EM YOKUM

BΘΠ

Opposite, top: Not even rain could dampen spirits at the 1961 Homecoming Bonfire. *Courtesy of the* Makio.

Opposite, bottom: An Ohio State Yokum chokes an Iowa victim as part of Beta Theta Pi's Homecoming decorations. *Courtesy of the* Makio.

Above: Turnabout is fair play. Proper young ladies assist their dates with their coats for the 1962 Golddiggers Dance. *Courtesy of the* Makio.

but that was about it. Instead of Greek Week, the annual Golddiggers Dance became the signature event for the winter quarter. For a twist on the traditional way of doing things, women invited men to the dance, which had been sponsored by WSGA since 1937. The women also voted on a Golddiggers King. The March 2 dance at the Ohio Union drew a crowd of 1,900—its largest ever.

Organizers built May Week '62 around the centennial of the 1862 Morrill Act, which created the land-grant college system. For some reason, that translated to a Frontier Days theme. Blessed with seasonably mild weather, the week was a resounding success. At the Wednesday Carnival, the five May Queen finalists were auctioned off to a group of about thirty "wildly cheering" men from Park Hall for thirty-four dollars. "The fate of the girls is not known at this time," the *Lantern* reported. Some 4,300

Junior Joe Yantis gets a bucket of water in the face as part of his initiation into Bucket and Dipper Junior Honorary during May Week 1962. *Courtesy of the* Makio.

ROTC cadets marched on May Day, while junior Gary Larson won the beard contest and freshman Erin Malley was named the May Week Queen. The May Week concert was a big hit, as described in the following section, and more than six thousand Buckeye faithful turned out for the red-and-white intra-squad scrimmage on Saturday.

SHOWTIME

Folk Music Reigns

The jazzy orchestrations of Stan Kenton and the harmonic stylings of the Four Freshmen faced a more competitive concert market in the early 1960s with the revival of folk music. College students across the country were drawn to the music's authenticity, so it wasn't surprising that Ohio Staters, a university-affiliated service organization that had a knack for nailing top-flight

Folk singer Joan Baez (*left*) hobnobs with two unidentified admirers. They are most likely representatives of Ohio Staters, who gave her the check she is holding. *Courtesy of the* Makio. Folk singer Phil Ochs (*right*) serenades free speech advocates on the Oval in the spring of 1965. *Courtesy of the* Lantern.

entertainment, entered the folk scene in a big way with Joan Baez. Named the "queen of U.S. folk musicians" by *Life* magazine, the twenty-one-year-old singer enthralled the Mershon crowd on May 4 with her crystal-clear voice and "majestic stage presence," said *Lantern* reviewer Diana Morse. The high point of the concert came when Baez asked the crowd to sing along with her on "Kumbaya," the popular campfire song that celebrates spiritual unity and personal fulfillment.

The Multitalented Phil Ochs

Before he played guitar and wrote music, and before he became a renowned protest singer, Phil Ochs reported for the *Lantern*. Reviewing the Mershon performance of Andres Segovia in January, who is considered the world's greatest guitarist, Ochs wrote, "Under the skilled hands of Segovia, the guitar loses its identity and become[s] a piano, a string ensemble, an entire orchestra. It is a part of him, and through him, it is a living part of the audience." Ochs set his sights on becoming the editor of the *Lantern*, but his campaign failed, and he dropped out of Ohio State and into musical history.

An Audrey Hepburn Moment

Columbus welcomed *Breakfast at Tiffany's* and Audrey Hepburn's party girl Holly Golightly on November 9 at the Lowe's Ohio Theatre downtown. The romantic comedy, based on Truman Capote's book of the same name, earned Hepburn an Academy Award nomination for best actress and became one of the iconic movies of the 1960s. The movie came to the campus-area State Theater in the first week in January 1962.

An advertisement for the Columbus opening of *Breakfast at Tiffany's*. *Courtesy of the* Lantern.

FASHION

Canvas and Madras

Canvas and madras emerged as the signature materials for those who aspired to be fashionable. The ubiquitous canvas tennis shoe came in a variety of pastels for women (men had their choice of white or white). Madras shorts, blouses and dresses were in style for women, and madras shirts, shorts and sport coats were in style for men. One snag was that because madras dyes tended to run, wearers needed to wash the clothing separately or have it dry-cleaned.

Madras is the message of this 1962 advertisement. *Courtesy of the* Lantern.

Women: The Price of Looking Good

The expectations of women changed dramatically during the 1960s, and the transition was not always smooth or easy. *Lantern* reporters took on the issue as well. Reporter Karen Groezinger described how the average Ohio State coed spent about ten hours a week on their hair and makeup, including washing and setting their hair twice a week. Jane Higgins elaborated on the ritual when she described how many women tried to sleep in awkward positions, including lying on their face or arm, to avoid the pain of brushes and rollers, which she said would "often leave dents in the scalp."

Marlene Gelfand tackled the question of why women attended college: Was it to get a mate or an education? She said the opinions of both men and women were divided. Gelfand quoted one coed, a junior in education, who expressed the dilemma by saying, "Girls just don't know what attitude to take. If they act like they are really eager to become married, they scare the boy away. If they express a negative attitude about marriage, saying 'No, not for me!' a boy will definitely agree. It does not work either way."

Curlers were part of the torture endured by women, but not men, in the early 1960s. *Courtesy of the* Makio.

PLACES

Happy Tenth Birthday

The Ohio Union was the epicenter of student activity since it opened in November 1951. For Ohio State's ten thousand commuting students, it was a home away from home and the classroom. And for the thousands of students in crowded dorms and rooming houses, it was a place to get away. The union also housed the offices of student organizations and enjoyed its status as the preferred venue for campus social events. The union's tenth birthday was celebrated with a candlelight dinner dance and the cutting of a cake shaped like the building.

The Ohio Union also hosted its first Las Vegas night in 1962. Just twenty-five cents bought one hundred dollars in phony money to play blackjack, chuck-a-luck and other games of chance. Las Vegas night proved popular and became one of the union's signature annual events.

Statistics released during the birthday party documented the union's impact. It served 4,330 meals a day in its four restaurants. Students bowled 575 games daily in its basement alleys, and nearly 1,000 students and

Above: The Ohio Union Tavern was a popular hangout. Here, sharply dressed senior Peter Alesch and freshman Karen Scott met for a study date.

Right: Freshman Joy Shepard (*left*) and junior Sandra Oxley (*right*) promote the first Las Vegas Night at the Ohio Union. *Courtesy of the* Lantern.

nonstudents attended various events daily, including fifty-seven scheduled dance parties annually. In total, the Ohio Union averaged 6,000 visitors a day—much more than the 3,500 daily visits to the Main Library. In a *Lantern* interview, Wendell Ellenwood, who served as the union's director from 1958 to 1983, called the social spot one of the "best in the country."

A Gathering Place for Eclectics

While the Ohio Union continued catering to the traditional student, a familiar fraternity bar gradually reinvented itself. Larry's began drawing an eclectic crowd of intellectuals and nonconformists—all by design. Larry Paoletti, the son of the original owner, created a welcoming environment for just about anyone who prized quiet, creative conversation over drinking and dancing. The relaxed atmosphere fostered talking and listening, poetry readings and chess matches, with jukebox tunes selected by Paoletti and occasional live music. Phil Ochs played there during the golden age of folk music in the early 1960s.

As the years passed, Larry's became the favored hangout of the growing campus counterculture. In a 1967 *Lantern* interview, manager Richard Christman had this to say about the bar's clientele: "We get pseudo-intellectuals, teenyboppers, grad students, a few North Complex undergrads and a substantial left-wing fringe." For a while, it appeared that Larry's would weather the changing times, but it was not to be. Larry's closed on December 27, 2008, leaving behind a fitting epitaph graffitied on a bathroom wall: "There's no place quite like Larry's."

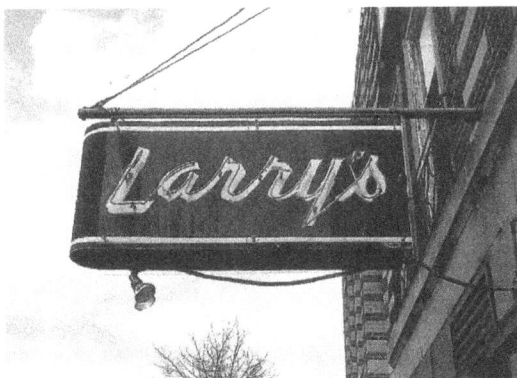

Larry's distinctive green sign.
Courtesy of Scott Arms.

BUCKEYE BITS

Spring Time Study Date

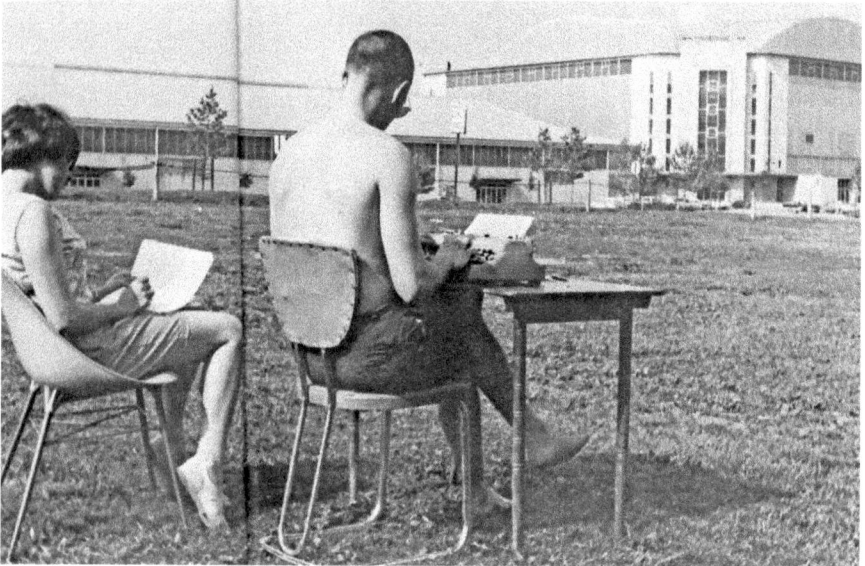

A mild spring day gave this enterprising couple an opportunity to get their work done and catch some sun. *Courtesy of the* Makio.

3

TOGA TIME

1962-63

Toga parties flourished, an iconic folk trio sang at Mershon Auditorium, Charbert's branched out, freakish rainfalls flooded High Street and fashion welcomed the big tease.

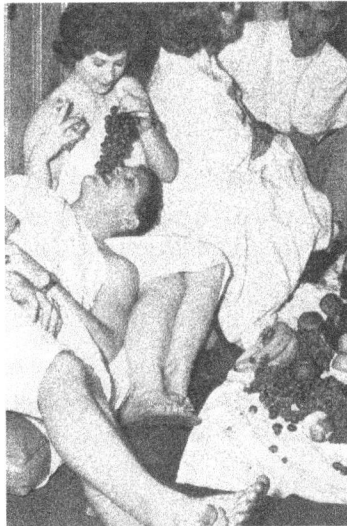

The couple on the left dances at the Pi Kappa Alpha Toga Party in April 1963, while the couples on the right celebrate the glory that was Rome at Delta Sigma Phi's Greeks Go Wild Party. *Courtesy of the* Makio.

PARTY TIME

All Hail Rome

Wrapped in white bedsheets, with sandals on their feet, students welcomed the dawning of the age of toga parties in a big way. Toga parties were immortalized by a fictional 1962 college in the 1978 movie *Animal House*. At Ohio State, the Pi Kappa Alpha fraternity sponsored the first registered toga party on April 6, 1963.

TRADITIONS

Missiles and Moochie

Students didn't let concern over the Cuban Missile Crisis and the world's closest brush with thermonuclear war dampen their spirits during Homecoming 1962. On the evening of the October 20, the night before the battle between the Buckeyes and the Northwestern Wildcats, 1,500 showed up at the Ohio Union to dance to the Glenn Miller Orchestra and listen to pianist Peter Nero. The next day, Ohio State lost, 18–14, and the missile crisis entered its sixth day.

The tradition of Christmas on Campus began in 1916 with the lighting of a Christmas tree on the Oval. By the mid-1950s, it had grown into a much more elaborate celebration that included a tree lighting and a candlelight dinner in the Ohio Union, a performance of Handel's *Messiah* by the university's orchestra and chorus in Mershon Auditorium and door-decorating contests in the living units. The celebration thrived through the 1960s but came to an end in the early 1970s due to falling attendance and lack of student interest.

The organizers of May Week created activities around the theme May Nineties, but Moochie, the 150-pound Saint Bernard mascot of the Alpha Epsilon Pi fraternity, stole the show. Frederick St. John, who paid $2.25 at the May Week charity auction for one day with Moochie, took her to meet his students at the Ohio State School for the Deaf in Columbus. "Everyone just loved her," St. John told the *Lantern*. "She is very well-behaved, and the kids…went wild over her." One of St. John's associates even bought the dog seven $0.15 hamburgers, which she wolfed down in no time.

These revelers added pyramid building to their Roman experience. *Courtesy of the* Makio.

No togas allowed. Thousands of students dressed up for the 1962 Homecoming Dance. *Courtesy of the* Makio.

Students sing carols as part of Christmas on Campus in December 1962—a particularly poignant celebration of life that came just two months after the Cuban Missile Crisis, which threatened nuclear armageddon. *Courtesy of the* Makio.

SHOWTIME

Located at the center of campus, near the corner of High Street and Fifteenth Avenue, Mershon Auditorium was regarded as one of the finest performance venues in the country after its completion in 1957. The acoustics were so good that an unamplified voice could be heard in each of the 3,072 seats, allowing Ohio State to attract a number of top-notch performers.

A Dragon Lives Forever

Folksingers Peter, Paul and Mary released "Puff, the Magic Dragon" in early 1963 and sang it to a sold-out Mershon Auditorium on April 10. Lines of students formed at the Mershon ticket office and snaked around the building on the first day of ticket sales. Just twenty-three hours later, all 3,100 tickets had been sold—a Mershon record. The *Lantern* published a photo of the concert but no review. The cutline said the crowd greeted the trio with spontaneous applause as they came onstage. Anchored by Mary Travers's powerful voice, Peter, Paul and Mary were already galvanizing a generation of young Americans while they were on their way to becoming one of the most influential sounds of the 1960s.

Left: Peter, Paul and Mary sing at Mershon in April. *Courtesy of* Lantern. *Right*: The actors and supporting cast of *West Side Story* on the Mershon stage. *Courtesy of the OSU Archives.*

A Really Big Show

Ohio State's theater department tackled the script, songs and accents of the popular Broadway musical that spawned the Academy Award–winning motion picture *West Side Story*. The movie about love and loss among rival gangs in New York City won the Best Picture Oscar in April 1962. Ohio State's production of the stage show opened thirteen months later. It was an ambitious undertaking, as not only were amateurs playing the roles owned by Rita Moreno and George Chakiris in the film version, but the production required fifteen scene changes and twelve different sets. A nearly sold-out crowd attended the premiere, and reviewers gushed that the audience loved it.

PLACES

Day of the Sacred Mushroom

The Sacred Mushroom, a basement coffeehouse across from the Ohio Union at 1716 North High, opened in 1959 as a jazz club. By the 1962–63 school year, it boasted an exciting mix of jazz, folk music and beat poetry. Artists who performed there included local talent, such as Phil Ochs, Chuck White and Nancy Wilson, along with national figures, like

The Sacred Mushroom, the epicenter of the campus folk music scene in the early 1960s. *Courtesy of the* Makio.

Della Reese and Eddie Harris. But the Mushroom did not last forever; it closed its doors for good in the spring of 1964, swept away by the surge of Beatlemania.

The Char-Bar Is Born

The Char-Bar opened its doors in 1962 at the corner of North High Street and East Seventeenth Avenue and quickly became a campus landmark. It initially operated as a nightclub, but with 3.2 percent beer on tap, it quickly morphed into a favorite undergraduate drinking spot, especially for the Greek community, whose houses were just east of High Street.

The Char-Bar was owned by Charles and Robert Gordon, brothers who came to Columbus after World War II and opened two campus eateries: Charbert's at 1912 North High in 1947 and another Charbert's on East Fifteenth Street, just off of High Street, the following year. The latter Charbert's, a tidy coffee-and-sandwich shop that was frequented by Greeks and students who lived in nearby rooming houses, earned the nickname Clean Charbert's. The High Street restaurant, on the other hand, functioned as a Las Vegas–style diner, open twenty-four hours a day with counter service. It drew a diverse clientele and eventually became known as Dirty Charbert's.

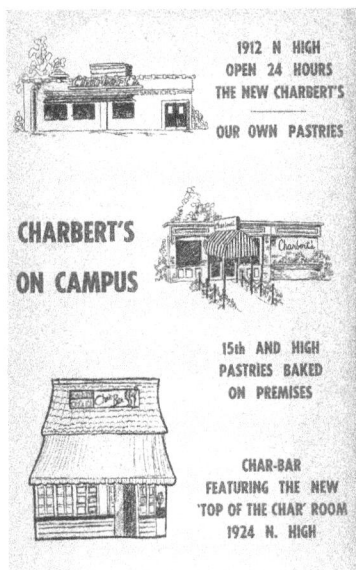

An advertisement for the two Charbert's restaurants and the Char-Bar. *Courtesy of the* Sundial.

The three businesses thrived during the 1960s but sputtered in the 1970s with the arrival of fast-food chain restaurants. Both Charbert's restaurant locations closed by the early 1980s. The Char-Bar hung on but suffered considerably after 1984, when the Ohio legislature changed the legal drinking age to twenty-one, effectively eliminating 3.2 percent beer. The campus Char-Bar closed in 1987, but a successor continues to operate in the Short North district.

Weather Woes

The skinny on the weather in Columbus is this: If you don't like it, wait twenty minutes, and it will change. Blame it on geography and topography; without the protection of mountains and large bodies of water, central Ohio is vulnerable to whatever blows in from the frigid North, the windswept Great Plains and the humid South. It's probably no coincidence that "Carmen Ohio," Ohio State's alma mater, mentions "summer's heat and winter's cold."

The winter of 1963 brought with it the decade's worst cold wave, and the spring and summer rains flooded North High Street. Speculation about the origins of the freakish weather gave rise to a conspiracy theory that

Winter's cold, and spring floods buffet the campus. *Courtesy of the* Makio.

the renewed testing of nuclear bombs had upset the atmosphere; however, scientists debunked the notion. Whatever the cause, students, faculty and staff trudged on.

FASHION

The Big Tease

Women on the lookout for the next new fashion trend kept a close eye on First Lady Jaqueline Kennedy, whose style and elegance captivated the nation. Women everywhere—from France to the banks of the Olentangy River—copied Jackie's big bouffant hairdo, which first drew attention at the 1961 Inaugural Ball. To achieve a bouffant like the First Lady's, women curled their hair, teased or backcombed it into a high pile, combed unteased hair over the pile and sprayed, sprayed, sprayed.

Fashion Jeans

Blue jeans, as popularized by actor James Dean in *Rebel Without a Cause*, became a college staple in the 1960s. They first became popular for men and later for women—but with a twist. They were more stylish than the slouchy workingman's blue denim pants, and they were worn pretty much everywhere casual clothes were allowed. By 1963, the Levi Strauss Company

TOGA TIME: 1962–63

Above: Bouffants galore! *Left to right*: stylishly coiffed fraternity sweethearts, Cheryl Lester, Diane Courtwright, Carol Harlow and Bonnie Hedges in 1963. *Courtesy of the* Makio.

Right: A Lazarus advertisement for white Levi's in the *Lantern. Courtesy of the* Lantern.

SATURDAY ONLY...AT LAZARUS GET HIT RECORD WITH WHITE LEVI'S

With each purchase of slim-fitting, good-looking White Levi's you will receive, without charge, a copy of the hit record, "White Levi's" by the Majorettes. Rugged White Levi's are durable cotton twill, in sizes 28 to 36 waist, 29 to 34 inseam........4.49

LAZARUS Downtown—University Shop—Second Floor
Also At Lazarus West Store

WHITE LEVI'S

COME TO

OHIO STATE!

SING OUT FOR

WHITE LEVI'S

SLIM FITS

Everybody's wearing trim, tapered, low-waisted LEVI'S Slim Fits—because everybody likes the long, lean, LEVI'S look. Cut from rugged twill, LEVI'S Slim Fits are equally at home in the classroom, on the campus, wherever young men get together.

branched out with white jeans for men, and Lazarus department store brought them to Columbus. Made of beige twill and pre-shrunk denim, white jeans exhibited the same rugged construction and durability as blue jeans. Originally pitched to men, white Levi's also became a favorite of college women.

BUCKEYE BITS

Oval Troubadours

These musically inclined students are probably not on their way to the library to study. *Courtesy of the* Makio.

4

A BRAND-NEW BEAT

1963-64

The Beatles conquered the United States in early 1964, but they didn't conquer Ohio State—at least not initially. Students were more interested in entertaining themselves with hootenannies, suggestive song lyrics, fast food, tainted meat scandals and sinister birds. But in the end, they succumbed like everyone else. The revolution had begun.

SHOWTIME

The Big Hoot

At the start of the 1963–64 school year, folk music hootenannies were the hottest musical events for people under thirty years old. The audiences surrounded the singers and became part of the show by clapping or singing along. The concept even spawned a television show when ABC started broadcasting hootenannies from college campuses across the country.

Ohio Staters, the service group that had brought Joan Baez and Peter, Paul and Mary to campus, stepped up to sponsor another great show. In January 1964, it announced that a hootenanny was coming—not to Mershon Auditorium, where musicians traditionally performed, but to the more spacious surroundings of St. John Arena. With popular folk group the New Christy Minstrels as the headliner, the Big Hoot would be one of

The dance step these people are performing isn't clear, but they seem to be enjoying themselves. *Courtesy of the* Makio.

the first musical events in the country to be held in a sports venue. Tickets included 504 "special" seats on the floor, which cost two dollars; other seats cost one dollar.

"The New York agency which is promoting this show will be watching the results very closely," said Ohio Staters spokesperson David Schumaker. "They're even sending an agent to help us," although they didn't need much help. While ticket sales were slow at first, all 11,200 seats had been sold by showtime on February 21. Another 800 seats were opened up behind the stage to meet additional demand. Musicians with the New Christy Minstrels told a *Lantern* reporter it was the second-largest crowd they'd ever played for. (The largest, presumably, was at Madison Square Garden in New York City.) The ten-member group put on a great show.

The irony of the hootenanny moment was not obvious at the time, but the concert proved to be a highwater mark for folk music. Just two weeks earlier, at a television studio in New York, the appearance of four young men from Liverpool, England, had captured the country's attention. The Beatles would soon sweep away everything that had gone before. At the same time, the Beatles' invasion would open doors to American folk artists, who flourished after a transformation to folk rockers.

The New Christy Minstrels perform at the first-ever pop concert at St. John Arena. Barry McGuire is in the center. *Courtesy of the* Makio.

The artists performing on the St. John stage that night included Barry Maquire and Larry Ramos of the New Christy Minstrels. McGuire later left the group and record the 1960s protest classic "Eve of Destruction." Ramos left shortly thereafter and took his banjo to California to join harmony rockers, The Association of "Along Come Mary" and "Cherish" fame. The warm-up group that night called themselves the Journeymen; it included John Phillips and Scot McKenzie. Phillips went on to write and record the folk-rock classic "California Dreamin'" as part of the Mamas and the Papas. Scott McKenzie went on to record the Summer of Love classic "San Francisco (Be Sure to Wear Flowers in Your Hair)," which was written for him by John Phillips.

Hello, Louis

Legendary trumpeter Louis Armstrong highlighted the Mershon season with a Valentine's Day concert on February 14. Armstrong and his six-person ensemble entertained a sold-out crowd with two and a half hours of blues and Dixieland jazz music. The following day, his rendition of "Hello,

Above: What British invasion?
The timeless Louis Armstrong
and his trumpet entertain a sold-
out and enthusiastic Mershon
Auditorium crowd in February
1964. *Courtesy of the* Makio.

Right: Patricia Landes and
Paul Telerski in the Strollers'
production of *The Night of the
Iguana. Courtesy of the* Makio.

Dolly," from the hit musical of the same name, appeared on the national record charts, where it remained for twenty-two weeks amid an avalanche of Beatles tunes.

The Mershon season also witnessed the revamped *Far Horizons* travel series, which kicked off on October 25 with a visit to Australia via a lavishly photographed and personally narrated color film. But interesting shows started appearing at other venues, too. The Strollers Dramatic Society presented Tennessee Williams's *The Night of the Iguana* at University Hall Theatre in May. *Lantern* reviewer Betsy Rich loved the production; she wrote, "Powerful performances of tortured compassion, searing pastorals, and poignant moments make *The Night of the Iguana* a vibrant, shocking, explicit probe of human loneliness."

An Offbeat Beat

Also in May, electronic music composer Karlheinz Stockhausen performed before a full house of the curious at Hughes Hall auditorium. They experienced a unique form of musical expression in which, among other things, the same note was never used more than once. Stockhausen began the concert by instructing his audience to close their eyes to feel the full effect of the music. *Lantern* reviewers described the reaction as "varied," which was probably an understatement. "Some people said the music hurt their ears, others said they didn't like it because they lost the security which other music gives them." But one gentleman, who seemed well on the way to the psychedelic era three years ahead of everyone else, claimed he "saw birds, butterflies and other animate objects." As for Stockhausen himself, he admitted he "could feel forces, but did not see anything."

Nude to the Moon

In the fall of 1963, attitudes about what was acceptable on movie screens were changing. While it would take a while for more adult-oriented fare to spread to local mainline movie houses, two campus-area "adult" venues, as well as some nearby theaters, were already courting the growing market of young people. The Little Art Theater at North High and Hudson Streets and the Indianola Theater just north of campus began advertising regularly

—Special Bargain Discount Ticket—

LITTLE ART
THEATER
2525 N. High at Hudson, Col., O.

Home of Unusual Adult Entertainment

50c DISCOUNT
with this coupon at
LITTLE ART THEATER
New Show Every Friday

GOOD ANY TIME OF DAY— **ADMIT 1**

The Little Art Theater attracted college students, but the artistic value of its "unusual adult entertainment," as touted in this *Lantern* advertisement from October 1963, was questionable. *Courtesy of the* Lantern.

in the *Lantern*, touting such masterpieces as *Nude on the Moon* and offering discount coupons for college students.

Two movies that appealed to college students premiered in the spring of 1964. *Tom Jones,* a bawdy comedy with Albert Finney philandering his way across the old English countryside, debuted at Hunts Cinestage on the north end of downtown in March. In April, Stanley Kubrick's dark comedy about nuclear Armageddon, *Dr. Strangelove; or, How I Learned to Stop Worrying and Love the Bomb*, came to the World Theater near the corner of High Street and Lane Avenue. World Theater featured more serious works, usually foreign films.

In July, the Indianola announced that it was switching from girlie films to serious art under the new name of Studio 35. Mrs. Frank A. Marzetti Jr., one of the owners, said that Ohio State students could buy a ticket for a double feature for just one dollar after showing a university fee card.

PARTY TIME

Beatlemania

Beatlemania was initially slow to capture the college crowd, but once it did, there was no turning back. By the spring of 1964, Beatle wannabes and lookalikes were everywhere.

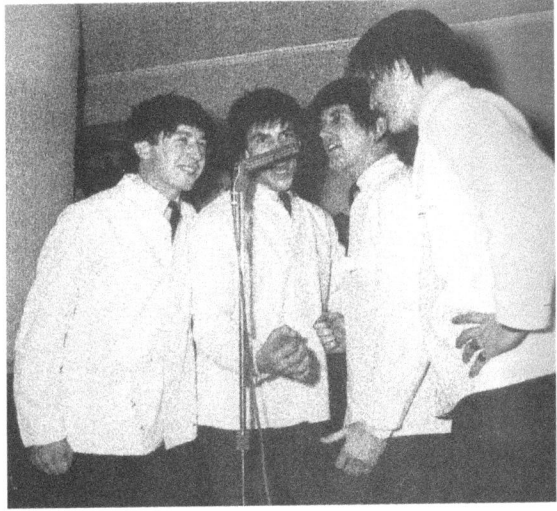

Right: The popularity of the Beatles sparked a growing number of impersonators at campus events *Courtesy of the* Makio.

Below: The Beatles also spawned a flood of would-be campus musicians who overwhelmed folk artists both in decibels and numbers. *Courtesy of the* Makio.

WCOL and the "Louie Louie" Phenomenon

Although Beatlemania dominated the music world in 1964, other artists were able to break through. Among them was the ultimate 1960s party band, the Seattle-based Kingsmen. The controversy surrounding the Kingsmen's hit "Louie Louie" grew out of a hurried recording session in May 1963. The band was one of several to record the song, and in the Kingsmen's version the words were somewhat indistinct—either by accident or design. Rumors soon spread that the lyrics were obscene. The *Lantern* put two reporters on the story to find out what was really going on.

They found two versions of the lyrics. The "bad lyrics" version, they determined—without explaining exactly why—had its roots in Siebert Hall, a women's residence hall. Ohio State conspirators claimed to have sent the

51

offensive lyrics to eight other universities. But these were not the "official" lyrics. The *Lantern* enlisted authority Steve Joos, program director for WCOL, to supply the "real" lyrics. At the time, WCOL was the only Columbus radio station to regularly play rock music. Joos was not about to take the song off the air. "Unless the lyrics are proven abusive, we will continue to play the record," he insisted. Joos contacted the Kingsmen's label, Wand Records in New York, and the *Lantern* reprinted the non-obscene version the company provided in its entirety.

Not everyone accepted the story. "I liked the song until I heard the bad words," claimed freshman Linda Powell. Junior Stacy Henderson opined, "I don't think it should be broadcast because the words come out pretty plain." Mary Lou Norton, a sophomore, was part of a group that did its own investigation. "We taped it off the radio and at slow speeds," she explained, "and at slow speeds, it sounds bad." Area record stores reported that they sold at least fifty of the singles in three or four days. A spokesperson for Turntable Records relayed one conversation: "One girl said she thought the record was terrible. But she bought it anyhow."

"Louie Louie" spent thirteen weeks on WCOL's Music Meter, and it even reached the coveted no. 1 spot on December 23, 1963. When it came to choosing Homecoming entertainment for the fall of 1964, the organizers proudly announced that the Kingsmen would perform at the Ohio Union.

TRADITIONS

Rolling Along

Despite the brand-new beat, some traditions did just fine. Planners succeeded in making Homecoming, Greek Week, and May Week bigger and better than ever.

Sixty-five housing units entered the Homecoming decorations competition, which was themed after Grimm's Fairy Tales. At the huge bonfire rally on Friday night, football coach Woody Hayes promised a "good game," and on Saturday afternoon, a record crowd of 84,712 watched Ohio State and Illinois, both undefeated, play to a 20–20 tie. That evening, the Highwaymen, of "Michael Row the Boat Ashore" fame, entertained at the Homecoming Dance along with the Richard Maltby Orchestra.

A May Week supper at the French Field House. *Courtesy of the* Makio.

Greek Week in February continued to grow in size and scope. The blood drive collected a record 1,034 pints. A talent show took place on Wednesday, the Lettermen performed in Mershon on Friday, chapters held exchange parties on Saturday and the tone turned serious on Sunday, when U.S. senator Strom Thurmond discussed defense issues at Mershon.

May Week's "Flapper Frolics" featured a Roaring Twenties theme and reached record highs in both student participation and profits, with more than $1,000 donated to charity. Events included initiations into honorary societies, a carnival on Wednesday night and May Day on Thursday, when classes were canceled, and students could play games on the Oval. May Day was followed by a supper at French Field House and a talent show in Mirror Lake Hollow. The evening ended with a crowd of four thousand jamming into the Ohio Union ballrooms to dance to the music of the Vanguards, a band described as a "twist and shout" group.

Celebrating Intramurals

Ohio State's intramural sports program, which was thriving under the twenty-six-year reign of retiring director L.G. Staley, celebrated its golden

These baseball players were among the six thousand men who participated in intramural sports in 1962 and 1963. *Courtesy of the* Makio.

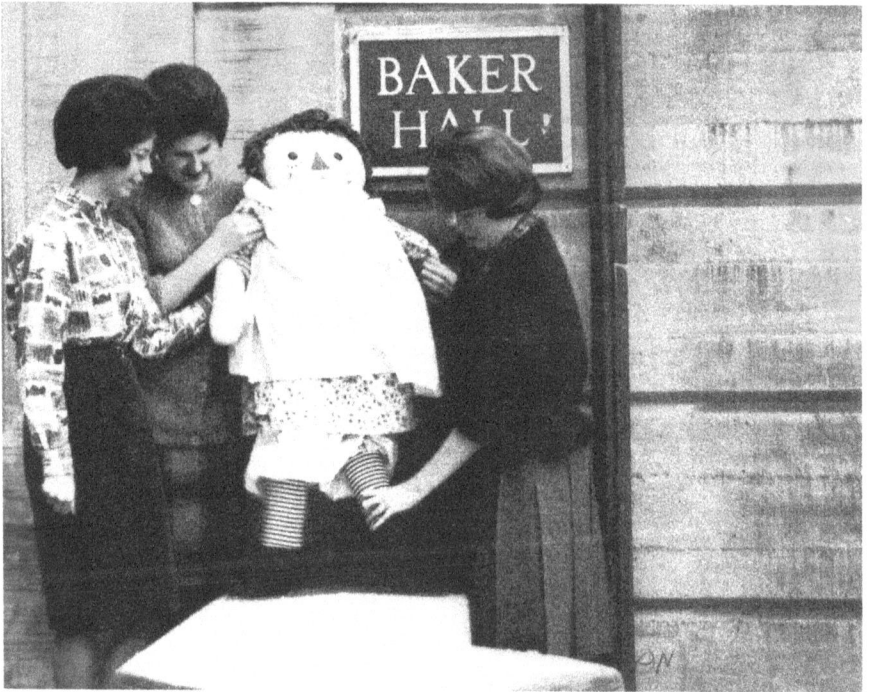

Linda Youtsey and Andi Zachary (*left*) and Kathy Lynch (*right*) celebrated West Baker Hall's triumph in the Buckianna Games. Youtsey and Zachary competed in badminton and Lynch competed in swimming. *Courtesy of the* Makio.

anniversary in 1964. In the fall of 1963, the university boasted that 6,000 individual male students, or about 30 percent of those eligible, had participated in intramurals the previous school year—an incredible rate for a voluntary activity. Winter basketball had been the most popular program, with 3,141 men playing on 361 teams. Touch football in the fall was next most popular program, with 2,500 participants on 175 teams, and it was followed by softball in the spring, with 2,225 men on 174 teams. Other intramural sports included golf, fencing, swimming, badminton and archery. Ohio State's program was very likely the largest in the country at the time.

But what about the 10,000 women students on campus? Title IX, which calls for equal opportunities in federally supported educational programs and activities, didn't exist yet. However, the university did make some effort to accommodate its female athletes. The women's physical education department and the Women's Residence Hall Council teamed up to sponsor the first Buckianna Games for those living in residence halls, sororities and rooming houses. Teams competed in eleven sports, including billiards, bowling, fencing, gymnastics, judo, riflery, swimming and volleyball. The 389 women who participated vied for an overall trophy, a huge Raggedy Ann doll, which West Baker Hall won.

ATHLETICS

Dream Teams' Last Hurrah

Ohio State's Dream Teams fought the good fight but continued to fall a little short. Nevertheless, they were able to get revenge on some longtime adversaries. After a mediocre start of 4–3–1, Woody Hayes's Buckeyes faced the Wolverines in a game that had been postponed a week after November 23, 1963, the day after John F. Kennedy was assassinated. Michigan was also having an off season, but the team had played well in its last three games and was favored to win the matchup. In a somber game, which was played in the Big House before a small crowd, the Buckeyes managed to exact some measure of satisfaction by beating the Wolverines 14–10.

As for the Buckeye Cagers, coach Fred Taylor said at his preseason press conference on November 3, "We're just fair….We're in the process of putting our game together." But when the Big Ten season started, the

Buckeyes got hot—very hot. They opened the season with a thrilling upset over third-ranked Michigan on February 3 before what the *Lantern* described as 12,789 "cheering, howling partisans." Gary Bradds scored forty-two points, but the clincher was guard Tommy Bowman's last-minute free throw after being fouled by Michigan's Cazzie Russell. Ohio State took the game 86–85.

After a string of victories, including two wins against their old nemesis Indiana, the Buckeyes took sole possession of the first-place position. All they had to do was dispense mediocre Michigan State at home on March 7. The fans who packed St. John Arena for what would be Bradds's last home game showed their appreciation with a standing ovation before things even started. But the Buckeyes didn't have it that night, and the Spartans pulled off a stunning 81–80 upset. That game left Ohio State and Michigan as co-champions with identical 11–3 records. The Wolverines were chosen to go to the finals because of their longtime absence, but at least Ohio State got the recognition of being the only Big Ten team to ever win five straight conference championships.

PLACES
Trouble for the South Berg

After more than thirty years, a legendary campus drinking spot endured a near-death experience. Located in the basement of 1532 North High Street, the South Heidelberg—along with its companion, the North Berg—was known for its subterranean atmosphere, which was created by low ceilings and catacomb-like recesses. But in the spring of 1964, the South Berg ended up on the Columbus police department's bad-boy list as a "trouble spot." After what was described as an "investigation" by the city's vice squad and the state liquor control agency, both recommended that the Berg's license not be renewed after it expired at the end of the school year. Deputy police chief Wayne Miller explained, "Either the owners are not handling their business properly, or the class of people going there is causing trouble."

The police and the liquor control agents also argued that the Berg contributed to an oversaturation of bars in the area. Friends of the Berg protested vigorously. If there were too many bars in the area, asked manager

The subterranean atmosphere at the North and South Bergs gave them a unique ambiance. Note the high-class light fixture on the ceiling. *Courtesy of the* Makio.

Jack Fox, why did the state issue three new liquor permits in the previous three years, including permits for the Char-Bar and the Library, both in 1962, and the Serene Lounge, just down the street, in January 1964? Fox also pointed out that there had been only two convictions at the South Berg over the previous eight years; one was given for serving a minor, and the other was given for possessing an illegal gambling device.

In the end, the Berg carried the day. All three members of the state liquor control board agreed with Fox and issued the license renewal. The South Berg continued operating as a favorite for south campus undergraduates for another thirty-four years. The bar was purchased in 2000 by Campus Partners, an organization that spearheaded renewal in the area, and it was torn down two years later.

New Players

Two major players debuted on the campus fast-food menu in 1963. One was a locally owned regional franchise with a gleaming, futuristic appearance. The other was a not-so-gleaming, one-of-a-kind place. Both thrived in the 1960s.

BBF, which stood for Burger Boy Food-O-Rama, moved into two locations on the east side of High Street, at Ninth Avenue and Eighteenth Avenue. The chain started in Columbus in 1961, and at its peak, it had forty-eight sites in Ohio, Kentucky and West Virginia. BBF featured a hip, space-age look, with a whirling satellite logo, and it offered fifteen-cent hamburgers, soft drinks and french fries. Invading the campus area two years before McDonald's, BBF soon established a loyal clientele of students. Both campus locations remained popular throughout the decade. But BBF seemed to lose its soul when it was sold to Borden in 1970. The quality of its food and its customer loyalty quickly declined, and the stores closed. Wendy's took over both BBF locations on High Street in the mid-1970s, and the company remains at the Eighteenth Avenue site today.

Clark and Judith Quisno opened Quisno's Sub House as a combination sandwich shop and pizzeria in 1963. Located at 9 Chittenden Avenue, just east of High Street, the small, dingy restaurant—technically not a fast-food place—had a few tables, surly employees and a floor that looked like it hadn't been swept in years. But it also had a good jukebox and the area's best subs. The restaurant's sixteen-inch New York–style subs, which had tasty hot buns, were made to order for dining in and carrying out. Quisno's thrived through the early 1980s, but the deterioration of south campus took its toll, and the restaurant left in 1988.

The Serene Lounge at 1560 North High Street, next to the Big Bear Bakery, joined the roster of campus drinking places in January. It featured something no other campus bar had at the time: a good dance floor. This made it an instant hit with the south campus dance crowd.

Fast-food paradise: BBF and Quisno's enter the scene. *Courtesy of the* Lantern.

Parking: Plans but No Solutions

At the end of spring quarter 1964, Ohio State released its long-awaited parking plan. The *Lantern* had worked itself into a near frenzy in anticipation of the plan. It ran a three-part series on parking the previous October, a two-part series in November and a four-part series when the report came out in June. The plan called for three new parking garages and a massive 6,500-space surface lot to be built on west campus immediately. It also called for longer-term steps for further study, including an underground parking garage beneath the Oval and the possibility of closing central campus to vehicles. The board of trustees approved the plan at its July 17 meeting. Included in the resolution was the authorization to proceed with the three garages, with the expectation they would be ready by the 1965 fall quarter.

The two years of studies also produced findings that say a lot about the habits of Ohio State's faculty, staff and students in the early 1960s. Here are some of them:

- The university had 17,626 registered cars in the 1963–64 school year, but it only had 10,000 parking spaces.
- An estimated 900 to 1,000 nonregistered vehicles tried to park on campus daily.

- Neil Avenue was the busiest route, with nine thousand to ten thousand vehicles daily, or almost sixteen per minute during the daytime. Half of those vehicles were coming to campus to park, and the others were passing through.
- The worst time to find a parking place was 11:00 a.m.
- On average, 55 percent of students walked to class, while 37 percent arrived in private cars. The remainder presumably rode bicycles, motorcycles or city buses.
- Altogether, students owned an estimated ten thousand cars.
- The typical student car was a 1958 Chevrolet sedan.
- Car ownership reflected the economic disparity between Greeks and independents. The typical fraternity or sorority member's car was three years newer than the average independent's, and it was much more likely to be a high-end sports car or convertible.

BUCKEYE BITS

Tainted Meat

Food service workers foisting tainted meat onto unsuspecting college students is a classic urban legend. The common thread is usually a tip from "someone in the know." The someone in Ohio State's case was a student worker who supposedly told the Men's Residence Halls Association that portions of two gangrenous cows had been used to make hamburger served at the south campus cafeterias in early April 1964.

The *Lantern* assigned a reporter to track down the source of the story. It apparently started when two cows in the university's meat processing laboratory were rejected by federal inspectors for abscesses. The two condemned carcasses were isolated in a locked room until they could be trucked to a rendering plant. They were never near the room where meat was prepared.

John Helwig, the chair of the Department of Veterinary Preventative Medicine, emphasized that the cows were condemned because of the abscesses, not gangrene. The firestorm quickly died away, but the question of what was in dorm food would continue to fuel conspiracy theories throughout the decade.

Hostile Birds

In the 1963 Alfred Hitchcock horror film *The Birds*, the residents of a small California town are set upon by hordes of malevolent birds. Ohio State students wondered if that was what was about happen to them in January 1964. "The trees around Lord Hall were loaded with screaming birds," one witness told the *Lantern*. "They had scenes just like this in *The Birds*."

Lantern reporter Nan Garrison set out to get the real story from Maurice L. Giltz, an associate professor of entomology and zoology. Giltz explained that about 2 million starlings, red-winged blackbirds, cowbirds and grackles had been descending on campus each evening. They were attracted by the grain in the university's agricultural fields, among other things, and they had, in fact, destroyed 75 percent of a cornfield the previous year. They also had no natural predators in the area.

Winter snow brought some relief, but in the spring, dead birds started turning up. Fifty were found in the Buckeye Grove behind the power plant in March. A month later, more dead birds and twenty-five dead fish were found at Mirror Lake. Investigators determined that the fatalities had been caused by the insecticide DDT, which had been sprayed on surrounding trees with the aim of protecting them from bark beetles. The DDT didn't stop the beetles, but it wreaked havoc on birds and fish. It is reflective of the times that, despite Ohio State's considerable expertise in the areas of agriculture and biology, no one seemed worried that the same insecticide that proved fatal to the birds and fish might also harm humans. DDT was not banned by the U.S. Environmental Protection Agency until 1972.

5

BUCKEYES A-GO-GO

1964-65

The first wave of baby boomers hit campus in the fall of 1964, swelling enrollment to thirty-four thousand—a large increase from twenty-four thousand just four years earlier. This growth meant crowded dorms, traffic jams and overfilled classes. But buoyed by a huge incoming freshman class of 6,928 fun-seekers, both traditional and nontraditional forms of student activity thrived. Functions such as Homecoming, Greek Week, Golddiggers and May Week had a good year, while the *"Playboy* philosophy" found a growing number of adherents, fashion-conscious students adopted a new look, and sidewalk surfing became the latest fad.

PARTY TIME

Bust Your Buns and Shake Your Bunny Tails

Even though they courted a different set of sensory experiences, both sidewalk surfing and *Playboy* parties appealed to many OSU students in the mid-1960s. The steady roar emanating from Mirror Lake Hollow in the spring of 1965 was not from thunder or machinery; it was the sound of steel wheels on asphalt—sidewalk surfing. Sidewalk surfers, or skateboarders, cruised on slabs of wood or aluminum about eighteen

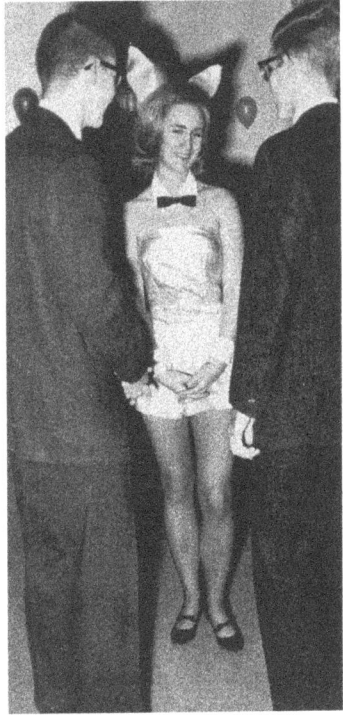

Favorite pastimes: Sidewalk Surfer (*left*) and Playboy Party (*right*). *Courtesy of the* Makio.

inches long with four pairs of skate wheels attached. Their goal was to guide themselves down hills and around turns at high speeds in a cross between skiing and surfing. The fad started in California and spread east, even producing an anthem from surf rockers Jan and Dean that included the memorable lyrics, "Bust your buns…and go sidewalk surfin' with me."

Sidewalk surfers overran the hilly area between Mirror Lake and the Ohio Union so completely that campus police worried they would bust the buns of innocent pedestrians trying to get to class. John Bonner, the executive dean for student relations, brokered a deal between the surfing community and the administration. In exchange for the sidewalk surfers being allowed to do their thing without interference from law enforcement, they agreed to restrict themselves to Mirror Lake Hollow between the hours of 7:00 and 10:30 p.m. on weeknights and between 12:00 and 10:30 p.m. on weekends. It seemed to work. The only recorded mishap involved two surfers who wiped out within fifteen minutes of each other on April

19. Helene Fracus and Walter Kuhlman, both freshmen, wound up in the emergency room with a broken ankle and a fractured leg, respectively. By the fall of 1965, interest had fallen off, and students moved on to other diversions, but skateboarding would make a comeback in the 1980s and remains popular today.

While some students engaged in sidewalk surfing, others celebrated a different subculture: the *Playboy* party. These events featured women costumed to resemble *Playboy* Bunnies, complete with ears, form-fitting outfits, tails and dark hose. Alpha Tau Omega at nearby Ohio Wesleyan University was the envy of fraternity men everywhere when it convinced Alpha Delta Pi sorority at Ohio State to send thirteen pledges dressed as Bunnies to act as servers at a banquet for members and their dates. Pledge trainer Melanie Besgrove, a friend of one of the Wesleyan men, received an honorary Playmate award and a stuffed bunny for her role in the event.

Because the *Playboy* parties were registered university social functions, they were not as licentious as one may assume. At least two adult chaperones were required on site, women had to be back in their residences by 2:00 a.m. at the latest and if the function was on university property (fraternity houses included), liquor was supposedly prohibited. Nevertheless, the growing popularity of the parties reflected a big cultural change among college-aged youth.

Playboy founder Hugh Hefner espoused more liberated sex and a lifestyle for men that included fine women, fine food and drink, fine clothes and high-class entertainment. He celebrated this outlook in his slick monthly magazine, which included serious writing accompanied by a color foldout of the Playmate of the month. The *Playboy* philosophy came under increasing attack by critics as being self-indulgent, pretentious and demeaning to women, but in the mid-1960s, the magazine continued to grow in popularity and influence.

It should come as no surprise that the Ohio Union newsstand reported that it sold each of its three hundred copies of *Playboy*'s October 1964 issue. Staff told the *Lantern* that customers seemed to be equally divided between men and women. Members of both sexes professed to be more interested in the articles and jokes than in the centerfold.

TRADITIONS

Entertainment for the Masses

Pointing to streets jammed with students and alumni, the largest number of Homecoming displays in university history (seventy), a big win over Wisconsin in the Horseshoe and a sell-out crowd that produced the largest dance in the history of the Ohio Union (featuring Count Basie and the Kingsmen), the *Lantern* declared Homecoming 1964 a success. The five-man folk group the Yeomen won the Greek Week talent show at Mershon on February 10, 1965. The group's members would go on to form the popular campus rock band the Ravens (see chapter six), which is still performing today. The usually staid Golddiggers Dance, a twenty-eight-year-old tradition, picked up the beat on March 6 with five rock bands in the Ohio Union ballrooms. Performers included Motown legend Smokey Robinson and California surf rockers the Rivieras (of "California Sun" fame). May Week's "Buckeye Badlands" featured 5,600 ROTC cadets marching, several thousand students playing games on the Oval, 7,000 attendees at the May Week supper, 5,500 at the talent show and 3,000 at the May Dance, which featured the perpetually popular Kingsmen.

Homecoming 1964: queen skits got more elaborate and flashier. *Courtesy of the* Makio.

SHOWTIME

Hugging the Middle of the Road

At a time when the electronically amplified guitars of British Invasion groups and American folk rockers dominated the nation's airwaves, Mershon Auditorium attracted an audience that found comfort in things that were more familiar. The result was a lineup that seemed more tuned to 1962, but concertgoers loved it. The season included sellout performances by calypso singer Harry Belafonte in October, folksingers the Kingston Trio in November and trumpeter Al Hirt in May.

Buckeyes and the Magic Box

While live performances continued to entertain, television strengthened its hold on young people, including college students who should have been spending their time studying. And what did Ohio State students like to watch on television? In winter quarter, the *Lantern* surveyed 1,132 students in an attempt to answer that question. *Peyton Place*, the first primetime soap opera, which involved a number of scandals in a New England town, placed first, with 332 votes, primarily from female students. *Combat*, the World War II anthology that featured Vic Morrow as the durable Sergeant Saunders, finished second, with 235 votes, mostly from male students. Also ranked highly were *The Fugitive, Bewitched* and *The Addams Family*. Two new rock-oriented shows, *Shindig* and *Hullabaloo*, also drew interest. Shockingly, 301 students claimed to be so wrapped up in their studies that they watched no television at all. The results of the *Lantern* poll were similar to those of a national poll of college students that was conducted for *Newsweek* that spring.

Beginning in the summer of 1964, Nejac's made a name for itself on campus by offering students portable televisions for rent for nine dollars a month with no down payment (about seventy dollars a month in today's prices). Nejac's eventually settled into a storefront near High and Eleventh Streets and offered music and stereo equipment until it closed in 1972.

Harry Belafonte was one of a series of older, more-established artists to perform at Mershon Auditorium while the British Invasion raged. *Courtesy of the* Makio,

Students find time to enjoy a television break (*left*). Note the rabbit ears antenna on top of the television; cable was still at least a decade away. *Courtesy of the* Makio. Nejac's (*right*) was the place to go for a television. *Courtesy of the* Lantern.

FASHION

The Flip Is the Look

Music wasn't the only thing changing in 1964 and 1965; students were sporting a new look. Skirts were shorter, hair was longer and the fun was just beginning. Sweaters were king, but they were no longer the cardigans of the early part of the decade; instead, V-necks and turtleneck pullovers ruled. About 250 students showed up for the first coed fashion show at the Park Hall lounge on October 19, which was sponsored jointly by Park and Baker Halls. Dorm residents were the models, and Marvin's Menswear and the University Shop provided the fashions. Navy, burgundy and camel were the colors of choice for men, and olive, bone and camel were the choice colors for women.

Other popular items included textured stockings and cutoff jeans for women and seersucker sport coats and wrinkle-resistant Levi's for men. Winter brought furry hats and high boots for women. Some men found the footwear sexy, but one male student told the *Lantern*, "I don't think much of these high boots. They remind me of cowboys, and I don't like to think of girls as cowboys."

Hairstyles defined much of the youth look of the 1960s, and midway through the decade, the hair was definitely longer. When *Newsweek* wanted a photogenic college student to model for the cover of its "Campus '65" issue, it chose Vicki Albright, a UCLA student and aspiring actress. Albright exuded just the right combination of freshness and self-confidence.

Female fashion plate 1965: this student was perfectly attired from head to toe, beginning with her penny loafers and textured stockings. Her pleated skirt rose to just above her knee. She was wearing a turtleneck sweater with a fraternity pin, and her hair was carefully flipped to just above her shoulders. *Courtesy of the* Makio.

She also sported the most popular hairstyle of the day: the flip. It featured hair parted to one side and combed over the top of the forehead, and the ends were flipped just above the shoulders. It didn't hurt if the hair

The flip is in! Six fraternity sweethearts from the pages of the 1965 *Makio* demonstrate the popularity of the flip. *Clockwise from the top*: junior Nancy Samson, freshman Joyce Gallogly, senior Marianne Wolfe, senior Kathy Lewis, freshman Patricia Brennan and freshman Susan Benson. *Courtesy of the* Makio.

was blond, even if that wasn't its natural color. That spring, the flip was everywhere, including Ohio State.

Also in 1964, male college students, especially freshmen, convinced themselves that English Leather aftershave was an aphrodisiac, so they thought, the more they used, the better. Anyone who entered an elevator in a men's dormitory on date night risked asphyxiation.

ATHLETICS

High Expectations

The football Buckeyes began the season ranked fifth nationally. "As far as coaching and having spirit, this is the best team we've had," boasted a beaming Woody Hayes. He was setting up for a classic showdown at the Rose Bowl against Michigan on November 21 in the Horseshoe. The game was sold out weeks in advance. Scalpers reported prices between $15 and $50 for single seats, or about $115 to $390 in today's prices. The Buckeyes (5–0 in the conference) had beaten the Wolverines (5–1) four times in a row and only needed a tie to go to Pasadena. A crowd of 84,645 braved below-freezing temperatures to witness what the *Lantern* described as the best Ohio State–Michigan matchup since the championship season of 1955.

Unfortunately, it was not Ohio State's day. Woody's team committed a very un-Woody–like six fumbles and never got past Michigan's fifty-yard line until late in the game. The Wolverines prevailed 10–0, and to add insult to injury, Michigan's two star players, quarterback Bob Timberlake and cornerback Dick Volk, were Ohio natives. A disappointed Hayes cut his postgame press conference short after five minutes and refused to allow any filming.

Low Expectations

For the first time in four years, basketball coach Fred Taylor began the season without All-American center Gary Bradds, who had graduated the year before. The Buckeyes headed into their last home game of the season against the Wolverines with a disappointing but expected 2–7 record. But with Michigan star Cazzie Russell on the bench with the flu, senior guard Dick Ricketts led the underdogs to a stunning 93–85 upset over the nation's second-ranked team, ending Michigan's title hopes. Taylor pulled Ricketts with five seconds remaining so that the 12,759 fans in attendance could give him a tremendous ovation, ending the season on a positive note.

No Expectations

Nobody expected much out of Marty Kurow's Buckeyes as the baseball season started. His team had been competitive during the last three years but had never notched a Big Ten championship, so why would this season have been different? But Ohio State managed to not only win the Big Ten title but soar though the regional finals to win a trip to the College World Series in Omaha. There, the Buckeyes lost in a 2–1 heartbreaker to the Arizona Sun Devils, a team that included future major-leaguers Rick Monday and Sal Bando. But the Buckeyes had nothing to be ashamed of, and they gave new meaning to the phrase "wait 'til next year."

Meanwhile, the men's lacrosse program provided the biggest surprise. The team drew two thousand fans to a match against Denison on May 19. They won 13–6 and moved into first place in the Midwest Lacrosse Association, and they went on to win the championship. Lacrosse was Ohio State's only championship sport in the 1964–65 school year.

No place for wimps: Ohio State's championship lacrosse team. *Courtesy of the* Makio.

PLACES

Pizza and More

Of the three student food groups—beer, pizza and burgers—pizza was the most pervasive. Pizza outlets of various stripes dotted the landscape around campus. National chains had yet to emerge, leaving the market open to a dizzying array of small businesses. Seventeen establishments advertised in the *Lantern* during the 1964–65 school year.

Who served the best pizza? Two places stood out so much that they didn't even need to advertise. C&G Pizza on the west side of High Street, between Tenth and Eleventh Avenues, was the south campus favorite. C&G felt like an undistinguished, dimly lit local bar with only one distinction—first-class, thick and cheesy homemade pizza. It lasted until 1974.

Farther up High Street, near Seventeenth Avenue, stood the Venetian. The Venetian was more like a full restaurant with a menu of Italian cuisine, but its piping-hot, thin-crust pizza with a unique cheese taste drew admirers from all over campus. In 1978, the Venetian had to vacate its High Street location for 22 East Frambes Avenue due to a rent dispute with the landlord. It thrived there for another decade.

The 1964–65 school year brought another popular establishment. On East Fifteenth Avenue, just behind Long's Bookstore, students found a unique menu at the Huddle, a combination coffeeshop, kosher deli and doughnut shop. It was a big favorite of occupants of the nearby fraternity houses.

Pizza to go! Two of the most popular campus-area shops in the fall of 1964. *Courtesy of the* Lantern.

BUCKEYE BITS

The Sundial's Moment

By the spring of 1965, the *Sundial*, Ohio State's student-run humor magazine, had been around for fifty-four years. It boasted prominent alumni staff members, including humorist James Thurber, cartoonist Milton Caniff and Broadway columnist Earl Wilson. Although it billed itself as the "world's funniest college magazine," the *Sundial* did not have the cachet that such a distinguished group of alumni would suggest. A high point for the magazine came when it managed to get itself banned by President Howard Bevis in 1944 after it featured a student leering at a buxom coed in its "Freshman Uplift" issue.

Things began to change for the magazine when Columbus native Robert L. Stine joined its staff in the fall of 1961 and when he took over as editor the following spring. Stine revamped the magazine into what one observer described as "sarcasm, satire, and sex." The *Sundial* was at its best when it was poking at the pomposity of those in power. The *Lantern*, the *Columbus Dispatch*, the Women's Self Government Association, the Greek system, the university's agricultural heritage and, of course, the administration were often the subjects of ridicule.

It took these *Sundial* staffers twenty minutes to realize the campus sundial was not a water fountain. Note the Big Farm sweatshirt the student on the left was wearing. Jovial Bob Stine stood beside him. *Courtesy of the* Makio.

73

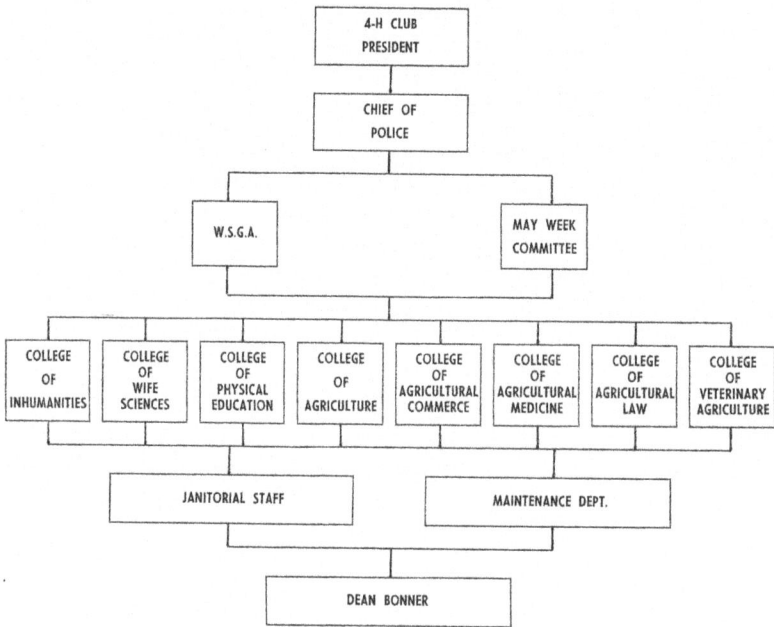

```
                    ┌──────────────┐
                    │  4-H CLUB    │
                    │  PRESIDENT   │
                    └──────────────┘
                    ┌──────────────┐
                    │  CHIEF OF    │
                    │   POLICE     │
                    └──────────────┘
        ┌──────────────┐        ┌──────────────┐
        │   W.S.G.A.   │        │  MAY WEEK    │
        │              │        │  COMMITTEE   │
        └──────────────┘        └──────────────┘
```

| COLLEGE OF INHUMANITIES | COLLEGE OF WIFE SCIENCES | COLLEGE OF PHYSICAL EDUCATION | COLLEGE OF AGRICULTURE | COLLEGE OF AGRICULTURAL COMMERCE | COLLEGE OF AGRICULTURAL MEDICINE | COLLEGE OF AGRICULTURAL LAW | COLLEGE OF VETERINARY AGRICULTURE |

```
        ┌──────────────┐        ┌──────────────┐
        │ JANITORIAL   │        │ MAINTENANCE  │
        │   STAFF      │        │    DEPT.     │
        └──────────────┘        └──────────────┘
                    ┌──────────────┐
                    │ DEAN BONNER  │
                    └──────────────┘
```

The *Sundial*'s interpretation of the university's power structure. *Courtesy of the* Sundial.

In the first half of 1965, Stine took the *Sundial* to new heights with two campaigns that fused biting satire with brilliant marketing. In February, Stine announced he was running for student body president as Jovial Bob Stine. In April, the *Sundial* began selling sweatshirts with the phrase "The Big Farm: Ohia State" stenciled across the front along with haystacks symbolizing the university. The popular sweatshirts were available in three colors in the *Sundial* office for only three dollars. The campaign paid off; *Sundial* sales reached a record eight thousand a month for twenty-five cents each. In May, the *Sundial* was voted one of the top-five humor magazines in the country by college humor magazine editors—the first (and only) time it would be so honored.

The *Sundial* fell on hard times after Stine graduated. Sales tapered off, and staffing and financial problems followed. The publications board finally shut the magazine down in 1968. Students have unsuccessfully tried to revive it since. Jovial Bob Stine, on the other hand, has made a successful career as R.L. Stine, author of hundreds of books in the children's horror genre, including the popular *Goosebumps* series.

6

LAND OF A THOUSAND DANCES

1965-66

D ance fever flourished in 1965 and 1966. Meanwhile, new traditions formed, an unlikely candidate dominated athletics, the London look took hold, new campus landmarks established themselves and Rhinos came and went.

PARTY TIME

Keep on Dancin'

Dancing was always a part of student culture, but nothing before or since has been comparable to the burst of primal energy that swept campus in the 1965–66 school year. Dances such as the Jerk, the Dog, the Swim, the Hitchhiker, the Monkey, the Frug, the Shake and the Watusi elbowed their way onto dance floors. The favorite dancing venues of students included dorm basements, recreation rooms in Greek houses, cafeterias and the Ohio Union's spacious ballrooms. For a while, even larger venues were called for. Parking lot dances had been around since the late 1950s, but in the period between 1965 and 1967, at least half a dozen of these giant events happened every year.

Lantern reporter Teddi Hilliard sought expert commentary from Jimmy Rawlins of Rawlins Dance Studio to make sense of it all. Rawlins explained that many of the new dances were actually "little step patterns" and that some of them involved specific arm motions. "They all overlap into something

She's got the beat—and then some. *Courtesy of the* Makio.

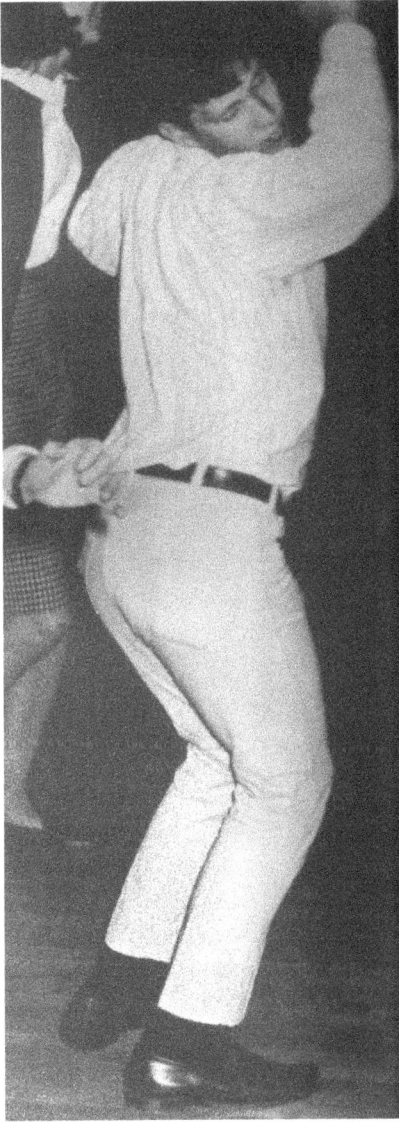

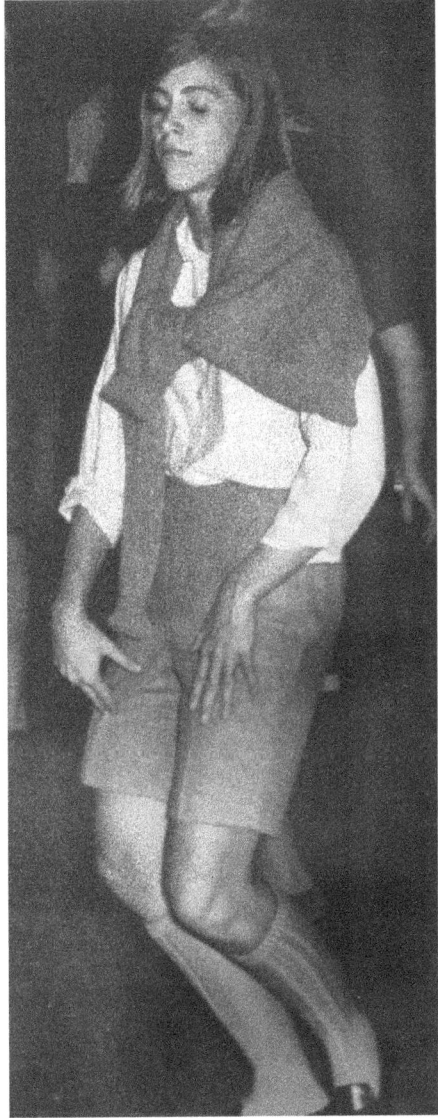

The dancer on the left appears to be demonstrating the Jerk, while the dancer on the right appears to be engaged in a séance. *Courtesy of the* Makio.

else, and a dance is a series of about 10 seconds of each variation," Hilliard wrote. Rawlins said that most of the steps had their roots in African and African American culture, including the appropriately named Watusi, which took its name from the Tutsi people of Africa.

The New BMOC

Campus rock bands thrived at the epicenter of this cultural whirlwind. Usually consisting of two or three electronically amplified guitars and drums, often with a keyboard and always with an animated lead singer, these bands spread across campus like modern-day Pied Pipers. These bands' frontmen took on celebrity status and became the new big men on campus—they were even bigger than student athletes.

More than two dozen rock bands gyrated on campus dance floors in the mid-1960s. The following are some of the most well-known campus rock bands from the 1960s:

- The Ravens, probably the most popular group, featured many members of the Yeomen (see chapter four). They boasted their own theme song, "Quoth the Raven Nevermore," along with lead singer, Little Stevie Stover's, classic rendition of "Shake a Tail Feather" (and he did). They also lasted longer than any other group and are still active today.
- The Sidewinders were led by 1967 Golddiggers King Jimmy Harris.

The new big men on campus. *Courtesy of the* Makio.

- The Majestics featured not one but two drummers who pounded out an unmistakable dance beat.
- Ivan and the Sabers often dressed in traditional Cossack garb. They operated out of Centerville and owned "Land of a Thousand Dances."
- The Gov'nors featured Stradley Hall's own Jimmy Fox on drums. Fox also played drums for Cleveland's Outsiders when they appeared on NBC-TV's Hullaballoo in the spring of 1966.

Other bands from this time period include Apocalypse, Cheerful Earful, Countdowns, Dantes, Electras, Fifth Order, Four O'Clock Balloon, Gears, Grym Reapers, Lord Nelson and Impressed Seamen, Lost Children, Mothers' Children, Peers, Raymond James, Rebounds, Sidewinders, Soul Merchants (Flying Machine) and Toads and Wild Bill Graham.

TRADITIONS

Something Borrowed

The Ohio State Marching Band represented many of the university's most cherished traditions. The Best Damn Band in the Land could trace its origins back to 1878, when it was a drum corps. The band's fabled ramp entrance into Ohio Stadium began in 1928, its conversion to an all-brass and percussion band came in 1934 and its signature script Ohio formation was first performed in 1936. By 1960, it was the largest all-brass marching band in the world. In 1965, the band consisted of 156 members (including 16 alternates), who had endured rigorous tryouts and paid more than $900 in today's currency for their uniforms.

In the fall of 1965, the marching band unwittingly stoked dance fever on campus with a tune that started as a one-off and became a tradition. The first performance of "Hang on Sloopy" came during the rain-soaked halftime show of the Ohio State–Illinois game. The date of the performance was October 9, but the arrangement had been in the works since August, when band arranger John Tatgenhorst heard the popular McCoys version of the song over the loudspeakers at the Ohio State Fair. He was intrigued with the song's unique sound and ran the idea of using it past band director Charles Spohn, who had replaced the legendary Jack Evans a little more than a year earlier. Spohn was still getting his bearings and wasn't eager to experiment, but Tatgenhorst won him over.

Script Ohio, circa 1965. *Courtesy of the* Makio.

With the exception of some dancing students in the freshman bleachers, very few of the 83,712 fans in attendance that Saturday seemed to notice the new arrangement—or so Tatgenhorst thought. A week later, in the midst of a game that was going badly for the Buckeyes, loyal fans who had followed the team to East Lansing for a matchup with Michigan State began chanting, "Sloopy, Sloopy, Sloopy!" So, Tatgenhorst and the band obliged from the sidelines. And that's how it went, again and again, game after game.

"Hang on Sloopy" became so popular that, at the end of the season, the marching band released a 45-rpm recording of the song and sold it in campus-area record stores. But five years after the song was added to the band's weekly playlist, Paul Droste, Spohn's successor as director, tried to pull it back a bit during the 1970 football season, citing his belief that folks would tire of singing and swaying week after week. Fan reaction was swift: "Sloopy" would stay. Twenty years after its debut at Ohio Stadium, "Hang on Sloopy" became the state's official rock song by order of the Ohio General Assembly. Ohio remains the only state with a designated rock song.

Something New

While "Sloopy" was becoming Ohio State's unofficial fight song, an unlikely figure was establishing itself as the school's official mascot. It all began with a contest sponsored by Ohio Staters; senior Ray Bourhis won with a papier-mâché model of an anthropomorphized buckeye. The model appeared at the Homecoming game to test reactions. Some fans complained that its big head was blocking their view, but as it was being removed from the stadium, other fans chanted, "We want the mascot!"

A reworked buckeye was constructed out of laminate and fiberglass over Styrofoam in the bowels of Drackett Tower for $250. Later that month, the new mascot had a name. Senior Kerry Reed came up with "Brutus the Buckeye" in yet another contest; Reed said he chose the name because Brutus means "heavy." Heavy or not, Brutus endeared himself to fans, and another tradition was born.

Brutus the Buckeye, circa 1965. *Courtesy of the OSU Archives.*

Something Blue

Not all traditions were equally cherished. Finals week, the five-day death march of exams at the end of each quarter, was variously described as a trauma, panic and a real grind by its student victims. Pulling all-nighters to cram was not unheard of. Libraries and cafeterias stayed open late, and social functions ceased. The University Health Service even blamed finals week for an uptick in cold sores and other maladies.

The song "We Gotta Get Out of This Place" by the British rock group the Animals premiered on WCOL in August 1965, and it quickly found its way onto jukeboxes and into the repertoire of campus bands. Propelled by a relentless bass line, Cynthia Weil and Barry Mann's angry lyrics and Eric Burdon's powerful lead vocals, the song became one of the classic protest songs of the 1960s. By the end of fall quarter in 1965, it had embedded itself as a student lament against finals week. Before long, it was adopted as an anthem by the American troops in Vietnam.

Something Dated

Other traditions rolled on much as they had before. Homecoming revelers partied with Buckeye Night at the Movies as the theme. Women townies entered a float for the first time ever and won. The Four Freshmen (whose last national hit had charted in May 1956) entertained at Mershon, while Les Elgart (who had last charted in 1956) and Joey Dee (who had last charted in 1961) played at the Ohio Union.

Greek Week featured Dave Brubeck (who had last charted in 1961), and the Golddiggers Dance featured Warren Covington (who had never charted). The May Week festivities, which had a Buckeye Big Top theme, broke attendance records. Clarinetist Pete Fountain (who had last charted in 1962) played the May Week concert at Mershon. In a sign of the times to come, fifteen students protested—peacefully—at the annual ROTC Review. Two students who weren't part of the protest group got themselves detained by university police for throwing water balloons at the cadets. Activists put a referendum on the student ballot to abolish student government. The referendum devolved into a debate over whether traditions such as Homecoming and May Week would be abolished with it. The referendum failed, but it kicked up an enormous controversy.

REVISED
FINAL EXAMINATION SCHEDULE
AUTUMN QUARTER 1965
December 11, 12, 13, 14, 15, 16

All classes reciting Mon., Wed. or Fri. at 8 a.m.	Thu. Dec. 16	8:00 a.m. to 10:00
All classes reciting Mon., Wed. or Fri. at 9 a.m.	Mon. Dec. 13	8:00 a.m. to 10:00
All classes reciting Mon., Wed. or Fri. at 10 a.m.	Tue. Dec. 14	8:00 a.m. to 10:00
All classes reciting Mon., Wed. or Fri. at 11 a.m.	Wed. Dec. 15	8:00 a.m. to 10:00
All classes reciting Mon., Wed. or Fri. at 12 noon	Sat. Dec. 11	8:00 a.m. to 10:00
All classes reciting Mon., Wed. or Fri. at 1 p.m.	Mon. Dec. 13	1:00 p.m. to 3:00
All classes reciting Mon., Wed. or Fri. at 2 p.m.	Thu. Dec. 16	1:00 p.m. to 3:00
All classes reciting Mon., Wed. or Fri. at 3 p.m.	Tue. Dec. 14	1:00 p.m. to 3:00
All classes reciting Mon., Wed. or Fri. at 4 p.m.	Wed. Dec. 15	6:00 p.m. to 8:00
All classes reciting Mon., Wed. or Fri. at 5 p.m.	Mon. Dec. 13	6:00 p.m. to 8:00
All classes reciting Mon., Wed. or Fri. at 6 p.m.	Tue. Dec. 14	6:00 p.m. to 8:00
All classes reciting Mon., Wed. or Fri. at 7 p.m.	Thu. Dec. 16	6:00 p.m. to 8:00
All classes reciting Mon., Wed. or Fri. at 8 p.m.	Mon. Dec. 13	8:00 p.m. to 10:00
All classes reciting Tue., Thu. or Sat. at 8 a.m.	Thu. Dec. 16	10:00 a.m. to 12:00
All classes reciting Tue., Thu. or Sat. at 9 a.m.	Mon. Dec. 13	10:00 a.m. to 12:00
All classes reciting Tue., Thu. or Sat. at 10 a.m.	Tue. Dec. 14	10:00 a.m. to 12:00
All classes reciting Tue., Thu. or Sat. at 11 a.m.	Wed. Dec. 15	10:00 a.m. to 12:00
All classes reciting Tue., Thu. or Sat. at 12 a.m.	Sat. Dec. 11	10:00 a.m. to 12:00
All classes reciting Tue. or Thu. at 1 p.m.	Mon. Dec. 13	3:00 p.m. to 5:00
All classes reciting Tue. or Thu. at 2 p.m.	Thu. Dec. 16	3:00 p.m. to 5:00
All classes reciting Tue. or Thu. at 3 p.m.	Tue. Dec. 14	3:00 p.m. to 5:00
All classes reciting Tue. or Thu. at 4 p.m.	Wed. Dec. 15	3:00 p.m. to 5:00
All classes reciting Tue. or Thu. at 5 p.m.	Tue. Dec. 14	8:00 p.m. to 10:00
All classes reciting Tue. or Thu. at 6 p.m.	Wed. Dec. 15	8:00 p.m. to 10:00
All classes reciting Tue. or Thu. at 7 p.m.	Thu. Dec. 16	8:00 p.m. to 10:00

In the case of classes meeting two or three times during the period, the day of the examination shall be determined by the instructor and announced to the class in advance of the examination period.

ALL EXAMINATIONS ARE ASSIGNED ACCORDING TO THE HOUR OF THE FIRST MEETING OF THE CLASS EACH WEEK: In courses of wholly laboratory work the examination must be held on the first laboratory hour in examination week. Conflicts should be reported at once to the Registrar.

Please notify the Registrar as soon as dates are chosen for examinations not scheduled above in order that there shall be no conflicts in room assignments.

All grade cards are due in the Office of the Registrar by 12:00 noon, Saturday, December 18, 1965. Grade reports are run by the staff working Saturday and Sunday. Grades turned in after the deadline are always reported as missing and usually result in serious complications. Professors are urged to turn in grades before the deadline if they are ready since hand sorting starts Thursday. Grades for graduating students are due at 12:00 noon, Thursday, December 9, 1965.

There are to be no final examinations outside the scheduled examination week except in the case of individual students who are graduating on December 17, 1965. Final examinations for all other students must be held within Examination Week. This is in accordance with the Rules and Regulations of the University Faculty.

ALL GRADE CARDS, OTHER THAN THOSE FOR STUDENTS GRADUATING, ARE DUE IN THE OFFICE OF THE REGISTRAR AT 12:00 NOON, SATURDAY, DECEMBER 18, 1965.

Office of the Registrar
October 21, 1965

Chamber of horrors: Fall Quarter 1965 finals schedule. *Courtesy of the* Lantern.

Nice work if you can get it: Ohio State president Novice Fawcett congratulates 1965 Homecoming Queen Sherri Phillian. *Courtesy of the* Makio.

SHOWTIME

Same Old Song

After bringing leading-edge entertainers, such as Joan Baez and Peter, Paul and Mary, to the Mershon stage, campus entertainment mavens continued to favor more traditional fare. Other Mershon artists had at least recently been on the pop charts, but they were still more likely to appeal to the students' parents than to the students themselves. Louis Armstrong returned for Greek Week 1966 on February 19. Piano duo Ferrante and Teicher, who had made their name with classics like the theme from *Exodus* (1960), played to a full house on April 6.

The year's most appreciative audience greeted Henry Mancini and his orchestra on December 3. According to *Lantern* reviewer Nancy deLong, the sellout crowd gave Mancini and his forty-piece orchestra a "tremendous ovation" when he opened with his signature rendition of "Moon River" from the 1961 movie *Breakfast at Tiffany's*. He also received standing ovations for three encores.

Doug Clark, with his group the Hot Nuts, was no Henry Mancini. Clark's ultimate party band featured risqué lyrics that got them banned from appearing on campus. Nevertheless, they were popular with college audiences and offered a raunchy four-hour show at the Crystal Ballroom at Buckeye Lake in April for only two dollars.

Somewhere, My Love (For a Price)

While the people who booked Ohio State's entertainment were becoming more conservative, those who made and distributed movies were moving in the opposite direction. As they were forced to take risks in order to draw people away from their television sets, MGM invested the then-unheard-of sum of $11 million in a movie it called the greatest thing since *Gone with the Wind*.

Doctor Zhivago premiered in downtown Columbus in May 1966 and promptly became the decade's most popular date-night movie. It went on to earn the studio five Academy Awards and $47 million, the highest box office intake for any movie of the decade aside from *The Sound of Music*. Even the *Lantern*, which missed the boat as often as not, declared that the movie was "impressive." But students without a lot of money had to wait for more than a year for the movie to come to a campus-area theater with cheaper admission prices.

Doctor Zhivago premiered in Columbus in May at Hunts Cinestage downtown. Two Saturday evening tickets totaled $5.50 (about $40.00 today). Sixteen months later, the film finally came to the State Theater on campus, where moviegoers could get two tickets for $2.00. The good old days weren't so cheap. *Courtesy of the* Lantern.

85

ATHLETICS

Ohio State Wins One

A Buckeye team finally won a national championship in 1966, but the team wasn't one of the usual suspects. The football squad finished with a respectable 7–2 record, including a victory over Michigan in the final game of the season, but it doomed its Rose Bowl chances when it was buried 32–7 by no. 1 Michigan State at Lansing in October. The basketball team had its worst season in Fred Taylor's eight years as coach, finishing with an embarrassing 11–13 record. But it was Marty Karow's baseball team that captured the limelight. They had come close the year before, but in 1966, they went all the way.

Hard-throwing right-hander Steve Arlin. *Courtesy of the* Makio.

After a 21–4 regular season record, the team triumphed 1–0 over a perennial favorite, the University of Southern California (USC), with a two-hitter by Steve Arlin; this victory got the Buckeyes into the College World Series. An 8–2 victory over Oklahoma State clinched the national championship. It was a team effort, of course, with catcher Chuck Brinkman, first baseman Russ Nagelson and outfielders Bo Rein and Ray Shoup making the all-tournament team, but it was fireball pitcher Arlin who dominated the diamond. As a sophomore in 1965, Arlin led the nation in strikeouts, and he finished the season with a 13–2 record. In 1966, he did even better and went 11–1, including two big wins over USC. Arlin left Ohio State that summer to go professional, and the Ohio State baseball team has never reached such heights again.

FASHION

The London Look

By 1966, many of the fashion statements that had given the decade its distinctive look had embedded themselves among Ohio State students. Longer hair, big earrings, bell-bottoms and the London look all were in play.

These two advertisements, which ran within one day of each other in April 1966, reflected the popular London look. The Lazarus advertisement claimed its Carnaby Street Shop was one of the first in the country and the only one in Ohio. If you had any money left after seeing the premiere of *Doctor Zhivago*, this would have been a good place to spend it. *Courtesy of the* Lantern.

These two fashion plates were captured by a *Makio* photographer on the Oval in the spring of 1966. Because they were not identified by name, it's not certain they were Ohio State students. But they definitely spent their money on cool clothes. *Courtesy of the* Makio

PLACES

A Big Player Arrives

The golden arches of McDonald's finally came to Ohio State in February, when the fifteen-cent hamburger palace settled into 1972 North High Street, between Seventeenth and Eighteenth Avenues. It was not the first fast-food chain on campus—BBF had already been there for three years (see chapter four)—but McDonald's became an instant hit with students. Rumors circulated that the High Street store grossed more than any McDonald's outlet in the country, with the exceptions of one in the Harlem neighborhood of New York City and one in Los Angeles. The success of McDonald's and other fast-food chains would hasten the ends of family-owned restaurants such as Charbert's, but there was no stopping progress.

Six weeks later, what became a long-lasting landmark arrived when the Bier Stube opened on the south end of campus at 1479 North High. The bar catered to upperclassmen and graduate students. It must have worked

those who know the score

rally at McDonald's

Before the game, or after, or both, the brightest people rally at McDonald's.
The chow's great. The prices are sensible. And the service is the fastest anywhere.
Look for the Golden Arches" — where quality starts fresh...every day."

McDonald's

1972 North High St.

Across from Arps Hall

OPEN NOW

Bier Stube

1479 N. High

would like to thank its customers for their continued patronage and ask anyone who hasn't stopped by — Do you know what you're missing?

The Bier Stube

- ● **Draft**
- ● **Free Parking**
- ● **Excellent Food**

Two campus stalwarts: the golden arches and the Bier Stube. *Courtesy of the* Lantern.

because the Bier Stube and the Varsity Club are the only campus bars from the 1960s that are still operating today. The Cockroach Coffee House at 47 East Twelfth Avenue, Luv A Go Go on North Fourth Street and College Classics Menswear Store on High Street, between Tenth and Eleventh Avenues, also opened during the 1965–66 school year. And locally owned Turntable Records became part of the Discount Records national chain.

Rhino's Rise and Fall

In February, frustrated university parking officials introduced a devilish device called the Rhino Immobilizer. The set of steel jaws could be clamped on a car or bike wheel to immobilize the vehicle until the driver owned up to their unpaid tickets. As one might expect, a strong negative reaction followed. Sylvan H. Kesilman, a graduate student in history, was Rhinoed for ten unpaid parking tickets, but with the help of a bystander, he was able to pry the device loose and throw it in his car before making his escape.

A game changer that failed: a Rhino Immobilizer is admired by Ohio State security chief Jim Webb and deputy chief Marion Curry. The unfortunate owner of the VW is not identified. *Courtesy of the* Lantern.

Campus police showed up at his apartment at 2:45 a.m. to arrest him for felony grand larceny and haul him downtown for booking. (The Rhino was worth eighty-five dollars, well over the fifty-dollar threshold for grand theft.) Kesilman maintained that he meant to bring the Rhino back to police headquarters. Five days later, the university dropped the charges.

In October 1966, officials announced that the Rhino had been removed from the enforcement arsenal. They claimed they were responding to concerns from drivers who said they might have to park illegally for a legitimate emergency; they feared losing the use of their cars at a critical time. Why personnel couldn't just remove the Rhino under such rare circumstances was not explained. Conspiracy theorists dwelled on the rumor that a Rhino's indiscreet application to a car that belonged to a member of the board of trustees was the real reason for the device's short life on campus.

BUCKEYE BITS

Make Your Own Kind of Music

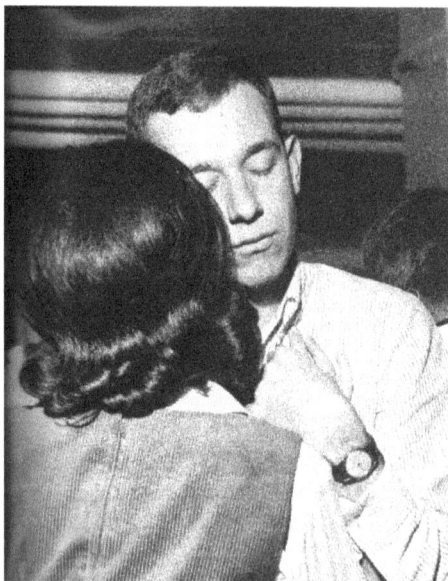

No fancy new dance steps were necessary for this dreamy couple as they embraced the timeless "double clutch." *Courtesy of the* Makio.

7

HAPPY TOGETHER

1966-67

T he counterculture grabbed the nation's attention in 1967, but Ohio State students weren't so sure about embracing it. While explosive enrollment growth opened new opportunities, it also produced serious overcrowding. Athletics had an off year, and "bazazz" was the fashion rage.

PARTY TIME

Counterculture: Not So Fast

Similar to the rise of the Beatles phenomenon, the hippie subculture took a while to thrive in straitlaced Columbus. In fact, the initial response to the movement was downright hostile. In March 1967, Larry's Bar decided that some nonconformists were too much to handle, even for that nonconformist mecca. Owner Larry Paoletti made a list of patrons who were not to be admitted because they had been involved in fistfights or were known to be underage. That list produced protests—even picketing—from some of the other patrons, but Paoletti stood his ground.

In July, Charbert's restaurant at 1912 North High, which was also known as Dirty Charbert's for its unconventional clientele, determined that it was time to rehabilitate its reputation. Co-owner Robert Gordon banned people

Above: This groovy couple had clearly embraced the counterculture, but not everyone else was on board—yet. *Courtesy of the* Makio.

Left: Hippies need not apply: people like this were banned from Charbert's and Larry's (*top*). *Courtesy of* OSU Monthly. The university area's first head shop, Trade Winds, opened in early 1967 at 1568 North High Street (*bottom*). The store sold water pipes, beads and incense and other artifacts that, while legal, were associated with the drug culture of the time. *Courtesy of the* Lantern.

Direct Purveyors of:
SANDALS; EARRINGS; INDIA PRINTS; SHEESHAM; TOGARI; FLOCATI; VASILI; CROFTERS; HOOKAS; NEW WATER PIPES; REED ORGANS; DRESSES; DROSTE; CURLING CAPS; INCENSE; BUDDHA PRAYER CANDLES; MAKONDO; 1933 AUBURN FLASHLIGHT; BUSTER KEATON'S NIGHTSTICK; WIDE MOD TIES

AND MUCH MORE
AT THE

TRADE WINDS
1568 N. High St.   294-2062
Mon.-Thurs. 11 a.m.-10 p.m., Fri. & Sat. 11 a.m.-11:30 p.m.

with long hair from entering the bar until they cleaned up and got a haircut. "Teenage hippies are now excluded," he said. "They don't go swimming, they don't play ball, they don't work, they don't study, they just come to Charbert's and freak out…taking up space and buying nothing."

But the major clash came over many hippies' recreational use of drugs. Hippie culture held that people should have the freedom to blow their minds as long as they didn't harm anyone else. Columbus law enforcement did not see it that way, and the war was on. Drug-related arrests soared.

Flash Mobs

The influx of thousands of new students made it easier for Ohio State to attract throngs of the curious for a variety of interesting events. The first big snowfalls had always triggered coed snowball fights across campus, and three inches of the white stuff got things going on the evening of November 29, 1966. A good-natured contest that started in the parking lot between Siebert and Stradley Halls turned into more of a brawl when a group of 200 or so traveled east along Fifteenth Avenue to pick a fight with the inhabitants of fraternity row. Up to about 350 students exchanged barrages. Although no one was injured, several windows were broken. Columbus police officers stood by but decided to not intervene to avoid sparking an even bigger confrontation. The fight ended on its own after about an hour.

An unusually mild week at the end of March incited a crowd-infused start to spring quarter. Six hundred north campus residents poured out of their dorms on the afternoon of March 30 to cheer on three unidentified Blackburn House residents who had made a slingshot out of fifteen feet of army surplus surgical tubing. They delighted spectators by firing water balloons at individuals down Woodruff Avenue, including one surprised motorist who was looking for a parking spot. Blackburn's dorm director put an end to the festivities at 7:00 p.m., citing quiet hours.

South campus residents had their own water balloon party on a warm Saturday afternoon three days later. It began when a group of male residents from nearby dorms started heaving balloons at bikini-clad Bradley and Paterson residents who were sunbathing on the roofs of their buildings. The women responded with a volley of their own, and the battle was on. It drew several hundred spectators and lasted most of the afternoon.

A similarly large turnout was not enough to save the YMCA–YWCA "computer dance" the same weekend. Participants were promised the names

Phi Delts, Sammys, Phi Gams

with Shindig Productions & Talent

Present: **THE PEERS**
THE MOTHER'S CHILDREN
THE SIDEWINDERS
THE LOST CHILDREN

The Biggest Parking Lot Dance Ever

WCOL Disc Jockey Bob Harrington Will Emcee

FRIDAY, MAY 5

Starting 8:30

Sammy House, 1962 Iuka

Everyone Is Welcome

FOLLOW THE LIGHT!

Three fraternities threw the "Biggest Parking Lot Dance Ever" in early May. *Courtesy of the* Lantern.

of three matches on an IBM card, but instead of mixing, the participants stood around listlessly, gawking at each other. *Lantern* reporter Kathy Redmond called it the "flop of the year."

The Phi Delta Theta, Sigma Alpha Mu and Phi Gamma Delta fraternities were more successful on Friday, May 5, when they sponsored what they billed as the Biggest Parking Lot Dance Ever at the Sammy House at 1962 Iuka Avenue. It featured four bands and a WCOL disc jockey as emcee.

TRADITIONS

The four major traditional events on campus all endured a degree of controversy—some of their own making, some not.

Homecoming: Ye Olde Entertainment

In October, the Homecoming committee took the unusual step of disqualifying Homecoming Queen candidate Kathy McQuilkin because her skit exceeded the seven-minute time limit. The sophomore theater major, who was a member of Kappa Alpha sorority and ran as an independent, appealed. She argued that she cut back the skit after being warned by Homecoming officials, but the sustained applause from the audience forced it into overtime. The traditions board agreed unanimously and reinstated her. She went on to win the whole thing.

Otherwise, the rest of Ye Olde Homecoming went on as planned, including performances from a lame collection of noncurrent entertainers. The Warren Covington Orchestra played again for the dance in both ballrooms. On Friday, the Homecoming Concert featured Chad Mitchell, who hadn't charted since 1963, when he was a member of the Chad Mitchell Trio, and the Harmonicats, a harmonica-playing group with a humorous bent that appealed to the over-forty crowd and whose first national hit, "Peg o' My Heart," had charted in 1947. They were joined by Cincinnati-area brothers

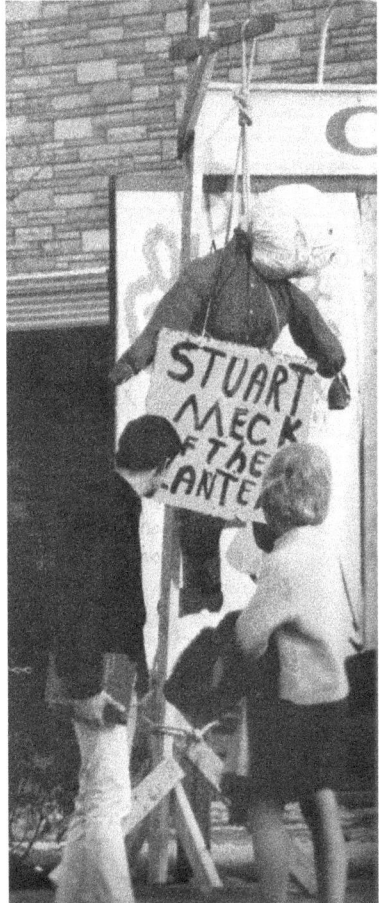

Homecoming Queen Kathy McQuilkin (*above*) had to fight for her crown, while Golddiggers supporters hung *Lantern* columnist Stuart Meck in effigy (*right*) after he was less than thrilled with the group's thirtieth anniversary dance. *Courtesy of the* Makio.

Gary and the Hornets, who were aged seven, eleven and fourteen. The boy band had actually charted recently with the eminently forgettable "Hi, Hi, Hazel," but they appealed more to the preteen crowd.

Greek Week: Never, My Love

Greek Week organizers pulled off a major coup when they corralled The Association to headline the Greek Week Concert. This California group's lush harmonies dominated the nation's pop charts in the second half of 1966 with "Along Comes Mary" and "Cherish." But the group's recording magic did not carry over to the Mershon stage the night of February 15. *Lantern* reviewer Michael Cothran called the concert a "miserable disappointment" that included a blaring lead guitar that drowned out the vocals, stale jokes and a poor selection of music. A good portion of the audience walked out before it was over.

The Greeks' domination of campus life had begun to erode in other ways. In May, a non-Greek was elected the Undergraduate Student Government president for the first time since direct elections began in 1962. And fraternities and sororities found that younger students were less interested in Greek life.

Golddiggers A-No-Go

The Golddiggers' thirtieth-anniversary dance on March 5, 1967, featured the Jimmy Dorsey Orchestra conducted by Lee Castle. With the theme Golddiggers a Go-Go, the even drew only five hundred people—just half of the previous year's attendance. It also drew a scathing review from *Lantern* columnist Stuart Meck, who called the skits "merciless mediocrity." A few of the remaining Golddiggers supporters hung Meck in effigy.

Mad, Mad May Week

"Mad, Mad, Mad, Mad" May Week went against the tide and turned out to be a financial and artistic success. Ten thousand students attended the May Week Carnival. A rare tie vote produced two May Queens. Pianists Ferrante and Teicher sold out their second concert at Mershon in just over a year.

A strong tradition: May Week pie throwing. *Courtesy of the* Makio.

SHOWTIME

Renaissance

While the traditional events, such as Homecoming and May Week, seemed incapable of attracting contemporary entertainers, the rest of campus was offering more exciting acts—some at new venues. The Place, a nightclub on Summit Street, featured Bob Seger and the Last Herd for two weeks in January. The South Campus Student Association, which was less than one year old, brought singer Dionne Warwick and Cincinnati rockers Them to the Ohio Union ballrooms in February. The Folk Music Club brought in legendary singer Pete Seeger in March, and it brought in experimental band the Blues Project in April.

Among the big players, Ohio Staters regained its mojo after wandering for two years and delivered California folk rockers the Mamas and the Papas to the Mershon stage for a concert on October 27. Just three years earlier, Papa John Phillips had played the Big Hoot in St. John Arena (see chapter four) as part of the Journeymen. The Mamas and the Papas, along with The

Folk singer Pete Seeger (*left*) at the Ohio Union ballrooms, and folk rockers the Mamas and the Papas (*above*) at Mershon. *Courtesy of the* Makio.

Association, were the hottest things going over the last nine months. Cheap seats for the Mamas and the Papas concert cost two dollars, but orchestra seats went for the previously unheard-of price of five dollars (thirty-five dollars in today's money). *Lantern* reviewer Karen Fiaone described the sold-out concert as "polished with controlled harmony."

On January 28, the Ohio Staters and Mershon combined forces to sponsor the biggest crowd-pleasers: the Four Seasons. Featuring the distinctive and piercing falsetto of lead signer Frankie Valli, the group had rocketed onto the charts with "Sherry" in 1962. Unlike many other American groups, the Jersey boys had survived the British Invasion, and young people kept buying their records. In the previous three years alone, they had placed eighteen of their songs in the top one hundred. Michael Cothran, again reviewing for the *Lantern*, said they "brought down the house" with three encores and three standing ovations.

Films: College Students Become a Market

As baby boomers reached young adulthood, filmmakers discovered a new market, and the campus enjoyed a number of innovative, smaller-budget films that appealed to college audiences. The underground cinema—films shot by independent amateur artists that were often designed to be viewed while under the influence of hallucinogens—received mixed receptions when they made an appearance in February 1967. Bruce Vilanch, the *Lantern*'s urbane critic, was not impressed. "The World Theater projection group vomited forth two and a half hours of underground movies Friday night," he wrote. "The films were, without question, the most insipid celluloid droppings ever to splatter against a screen." But someone must have liked them because the World kept showing them, and they were eventually supplemented with psychedelic light shows. Vilanch went on to have a successful career in Hollywood as a writer and actor.

Underground Cinema (*above*) came to campus in February. *Courtesy of the* Lantern. These partiers (*right*) were more interested in partying the traditional way. *Courtesy of the* Makio.

PLACES

The Law of Large Numbers

It's hard to believe that students did any studying between partying, eating pizza, being part of flash mobs and looking for parking spaces—but most of them did. In fact, the university struggled with where to put all those who were seeking quiet places to hit the books. To many, the best refuge was a quiet corner in the stately Main Library, but by the mid-1960s, those were increasingly hard to find.

While growing enrollment numbers created all kinds of crowding problems, the addition of thousands of students with discretionary income attracted new entrepreneurs and venues that wanted to help them enjoy themselves. University City Cinema opened its doors on November 16 in a shopping center on Olentangy River Road, northwest of campus. It was not within walking distance for most students, but those who managed to get there could enjoy first-run movies. The theater continued to show movies for twenty-five years until it was demolished to make room for an Applebee's restaurant in 1991.

The Bistro, a shiny nightclub located just up Olentangy River Road from University City, opened its doors that fall. Catering to both Ohio State students and the young people who were working on Columbus's growing northwest side, the club thrived as a popular hangout. It was known for bringing promising young talent to the campus area. Despite its promising start, the Bistro folded in 1976, and the site is now a hotel.

Spring concerts in Mirror Lake Hollow had been a tradition since 1929. *Courtesy of the* Makio.

Also joining the roster during the 1966–67 school year were a much-needed candy and ice cream store for north campus (Gordon's at 2197 North High) and the campus's first pizza chain, Pizza Hut, right across the street. South campus gained two rowdy new bars, Crazy Eye at 1434 North High and the Travel Agency at High and Eleventh Avenue.

ATHLETICS

In Retreat

In a disappointing year for athletics, Woody Hayes won his one hundredth game, but that about the only thing that happened. The football team finished with a 4–5 record, including a loss to hated Michigan. Despite the efforts of star center Bill Hosket, the basketball Buckeyes had a 13–11 record. The reigning national championship baseball team managed to win the Big Ten championship, even without Steve Arlin, but they were vanquished in the first round of the national playoffs. Students got more bad news in the spring when the athletics department, citing inflation, got approval to raise the student activity fee from twelve to fourteen dollars, the first increase since 1956.

One piece of good news did emerge when the university decided to double the size of Block O from 700 to 1,400 students for the 1967 season. Founded in 1938, Block O is the official Buckeye cheering section; supporters there are adept at using synchronized flash card routines to support the home

The Block O cheering section expanded in 1966. *Courtesy of the* Makio.

team. Block O's location in Ohio Stadium was also moved from between the thirty- and forty-yard lines to a location high in the bleachers on the closed end of the stadium to facilitate better television coverage.

FASHION

The Age of Bazazz

Bazazz—meaning bright and offbeat colors—is how the organizers of the Panhellenic Holiday Fashion Show described what lay ahead in 1967. At the same time, the London look still dominated as new fads were added to the tapestry. Military-style gear, such as navy pea coats and CPO jackets, were in. Knickers and saddle shoes also sprouted among fashionistas.

GO....
GO....
GO....
CPO

The wool CPO . . .
AVAILABLE THIS SEASON IN THE BASIC SOLID COLORS
(BURGUNDY, NAVY, OLIVE)
PLUS BOLD NEW PLAIDS AND HERRINGBONES
FROM
$9.95

Marvin's MEN'S WEAR
1872 N. HIGH AT 16th

A MEMBER OF THE NATION'S LARGEST GROUP OF APPAREL STORES CATERING EXCLUSIVELY TO COLLEGE STUDENTS

OUR NAVY PEA COAT
Breaks The Wind!
100% WOOL
Comes In All Sizes
$15.95

The University Shop
FOR WOMEN
18 E 15th Avenue
At Corner of High
294-4074

Left: This popular party dress featured alternating stripes of bold gold and bright crimson. Other popular colors included magnetic blue, fluorescent green and deep purple. *Courtesy of the* Makio.

Middle and right: Two mid-1960s must-haves: A navy pea coat and a CPO jacket (*respectively*). *Courtesy of the* Lantern.

8
LET IT ALL HANG OUT

1967-68

As war abroad and violence at home split the country apart, young people gravitated toward the counterculture. Traditions came under assault. Artists pushed past previously accepted boundaries, and fashion became a political statement.

TRADITIONS

In times of great turmoil, traditions can serve as a bulwark against further fracturing of a community or society. During the 1967–68 school year, many traditions at Ohio State struggled to stay relevant.

Ho-Hum Homecoming

The Tales of Tomorrow Homecoming did not get off to a good start. On October 24, three days before Homecoming Weekend, *Lantern* arts and entertainment editor, Bruce Vilanch, fired off a critique of what he believed was likely to be a boring weekend. He wrote what many had been thinking:

> *On Friday night, well-scrubbed couples will file dutifully into Mershon Auditorium to sit through another unbelievably mediocre entertainment*

Flower power invaded the Oval in the spring of 1968. *Courtesy of the* Makio.

presentation. This year's will star the Lettermen, whose last hit record must have been recorded several salary cuts ago. Si Zentner, whose "Up a Lazy River" has been around since Central Standard Time, will blare out. Jimmie Harris and the Sidewinders, home-grown boys, will be the best act of the evening. Afterwards, everyone will wonder why a school of 40,000 cannot get performers other than washed-out rock and roll groups and bands whose style is reminiscent of the rippling rhythms of the Second World War.

On Thursday, Homecoming Eve, a monsoon swept across campus, leaving parade floats a tangled mess of bent chicken wire, dripping papier-mâché and shredded tissue paper. On a gloomy Saturday afternoon, the football team did its part by losing in a fumble-fest to unranked Illinois.

But in the end, traditional Homecoming triumphed. A spirited crowd showed up for the Friday pep rally. The Lettermen sold out both shows at Mershon and entertained a well-scrubbed and content crowd of Ohio State faithful. Si Zentner sold out his dance at the Ohio Union, and nearly ninety thousand fans, the second-largest crowd of the year, turned out for the football game.

Other Shows Go On

Greek Week thrived as well. The Mershon pop concert on February 14 featured the blue-eyed soul of the Righteous Brothers and the country twang of Glen Campbell. No one walked out. Greeks also donated one thousand pints of blood.

The Golddiggers Dance took another hit from hung-in-effigy *Lantern* columnist Stuart Meck, who called it a "pseudo-event." The group had decided to stick with local entertainment, including the ubiquitous Jimmy Harris and the Sidewinders. Attendance figures were not announced.

Up to this point, May Week had remained relatively free of the controversies that were dogging other events, but it took its turn in the tank. First, a group of unhappy ROTC supporters petitioned the administration to reverse its decision to move the traditional ceremony from the Oval to the intramural fields, west of the hospital (allegedly for space reasons). Rain forced the ceremony into Mershon Auditorium. A small army of state highway patrol officers provided security inside the building, while pro- and anti-ROTC crowds mixed it up outside, throwing eggs and firecrackers at each other. By some miracle, no one was injured. An attempt at ballot box stuffing got two May Queen candidates disqualified by the traditions board, and rain dampened spirits throughout much of the outdoor activities.

The threat of rain did limit these students' enthusiasm for the May Week Bed Race. *Courtesy of the* Makio.

SHOWTIME

The Arrival of Acid Rock

While the organizers of traditional events continued to celebrate the bygone days before the Beatles, other actors on and off campus moved in. The North and South Campus Student Associations pooled $5,000 in activity fees to guarantee that one of rock's hottest acts would come to campus. The gamble paid off when all 3,100 tickets were sold for the November 29 concert by San Francisco acid rockers Jefferson Airplane. Playing selections mainly from their now-classic *Surrealistic Pillow* album, Grace Slick and her bandmates roused the Mershon audience with a decibel level that had not been equaled since the Detroit Symphony's performance of "Ride of the Valkyries" in 1961.

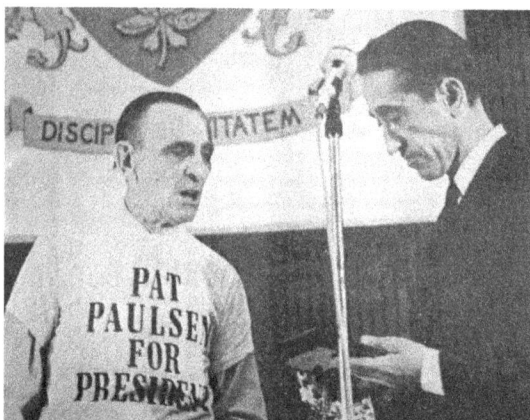

Left: Comedian Pat Paulson and Columbus mayor M.E. Sensenbrenner clown around. *Courtesy of the* Lantern.

Below: Feed your head: Jefferson Airplane rocked at Mershon in November. *Courtesy of the* Makio.

Other artists who played on or near campus included Kenny Rogers and the First Edition, who performed at the Bistro in October, and Cleveland's Outsiders, who performed at the Draught House in May. Pat Paulsen, a regular on the popular television show *The Smothers Brothers Comedy Hour,* visited campus on May 7 as part of his pseudo-campaign for U.S. president. Students cheered Columbus mayor M.E. Sensenbrenner when he showed up in a "Pat Paulsen for president" T-shirt and gave the comedian a key to the city.

More Psychedelia

Jimi Hendrix's March 3 appearance at Veterans Memorial in downtown Columbus featured the legendary guitarist and a psychedelic light show, along with the Dantes and Four O'Clock Balloon. The Dantes were regarded as the best local band in the mid-1960s; they played a lot of Byrds and Rolling Stones covers as well as their own tunes. One of the band's original songs, "Can't Get Enough of Your Love," even made it onto WCOL's top forty list.

Four O'Clock Balloon became the premier campus psychedelic band of the late 1960s. The group featured five current and former Ohio State students—lead singer Wayne Sheppard, singer Hazel Wiget, rhythm guitarist Geoff Robinson, drummer Jack White, and sound and light coordinator John Geyer—along with high school student Roger Alton on lead guitar. Four O'Clock Balloon headlined the Celebration of Life Concert on April 14. Although many students were away for Easter, several hundred gathered to groove at one of the Oval's first outdoor rock concerts.

Jimi Hendrix shared the stage with local bands the Dantes and Four O'Clock Balloon at Vets Memorial downtown in March. *Courtesy of the* Makio.

Where Have You Gone, Joe DiMaggio?

The 1967–68 school year witnessed the growing popularity of movies that had something to say. Two did particularly well, especially among college students. Arthur Penn's *Bonnie and Clyde* hit Columbus in October. Starring Warren Beatty and Faye Dunaway, the tale of the real-life Depression-era bank robbers became the fourth-highest-grossing picture of the year. Bruce Vilanch reviewed the movie for the *Lantern* and called it a "significant social commentary." He concluded, "You must see it....It is upsetting, nauseating, hilarious and thoroughly American. But your mother will not like it at all."

Four months later, the year's biggest box office hit premiered. *The Graduate*, starring Dustin Hoffman as an aimless young man, won both critical and popular acclaim. *Lantern* reviewer Jeff Tannenbaum began by praising the movie, which he said was "extremely funny" with "brilliant acting, photography and direction," but he faulted it for being "too obvious" with its message.

What both films had in common was an antihero who was at odds with the social norms of the day. They also reflected a critical view of authority figures, like the police in *Bonnie and Clyde* and the parents in *The Graduate*.

Moviemakers tapped into the theme of rebellion against authority figures in their films targeted at young people. *Courtesy of the* Lantern.

Hollywood movies always speak more to the era in which they were made than to the era in which they are set. And as the country descended into the darkness of the Vietnam War and violence at home, the nation's authority figures lost credibility, particularly among young people.

PARTY TIME

Beer Time

By 1968, the tradition of throwing elaborately themed parties seemed to be on the way out as students increasingly sought other pursuits. Drugs were part of the reason this tradition waned. In December, Columbus police busted two Ohio State students and a third person for being in possession of the largest marijuana stash in the city's history. However, alcohol remained the party substance of choice for most students. Under Ohio law, persons who were over eighteen years old but under twenty-one could drink 3.2 percent beer. Adults who were twenty-one years old and over could imbibe the harder stuff. But if they lived in university housing (including dorms and fraternity and sorority houses), they were prohibited from having any liquor in their living units. If they lived off campus in an apartment, which was the choice of more and more students, they could do what they wanted when they wanted. Many saw this as unfairly discriminatory and began campaigning to change it.

In January, the Council of Fraternity Presidents proposed to the Council on Student Affairs that residents of fraternity houses be allowed to consume 3.2 beer on the premises if their individual chapters elected to allow it. Dorm residents followed shortly thereafter. The residence halls associations for north, south and west campus combined forces to put a referendum on the ballot in February. It passed by a lopsided two-to-one majority with a relatively high voter turnout of 49 percent.

Ohio State's trustees took up the topic at their July meeting. They unanimously turned down both the fraternity and residence hall proposals, and they based their decision, at least in part, around university president Novice Fawcett's concern over the potential impact on students who didn't want a living environment where alcohol was freely available. With a rare split vote, the trustees did approve alcohol in the Faculty Club after 5:00 p.m. and in the Ohio Union.

Beer at the South Berg. Students hoped to get approval to serve beer in living units, but they were turned down. *Courtesy of the* Makio.

Sex and the Single College Student

While Ohio State was reluctant to give students more freedom to drink alcoholic beverages, other parts of *in loco parentis* (the doctrine that said the university was required to take the place of students' parents when they were away at college) were already on their way out. Within the last year, dress rules for the cafeterias had been abandoned entirely, as had the restrictions against women staying overnight in area hotels and motels. Curfews were abolished for senior and junior women, and these women were no longer prohibited from living in apartments. In March, the Council on Student Affairs did away with the rule requiring chaperones at social functions, and it became effective in the fall of 1968. All of this new freedom also meant that students had more opportunities to exercise their hormones.

For most of the 1960s, students living in dorms, Greek houses and rooming houses were not allowed to have vistors of the opposite sex in living areas unless they were part of a university-approved open house. The open houses were usually limited to one to two hours, and bedroom doors were required to remain open. Couples were also required to have four feet on the floor at

To be young and in love—sixties style (*left*). No more four on the floor (*right*). *Courtesy of the* Makio.

all times, but as the accompanying photograph shows, an increasing number of others obviously didn't feel compelled to observe that rule.

Associate professor Nancy Clatworthy was what students would later call a rock star. She had a PhD, and she was a wife, a mother of five and a licensed pilot who taught an enormously popular sociology course called Factors in a Successful Marriage. Although she belonged to their parents' generation, students trusted her. In fact, she ended up counseling many of them. So, when she was the featured speaker at a November seminar on sex that was sponsored by the student assembly, people listened. She supported students' rights to make their own choices and to have access to birth control information, but she also encouraged them to make good decisions. "College boys are mostly looking for sex, while girls are looking for love," she said. "Too many girls trade in the stuffed teddy bear on their bed for a boy without realizing what they are getting into."

ATHLETICS

Woody: Is the Magic Gone?

In the fall of 1967, Woody Hayes's football teams had not been good enough to be considered for postseason play since the Rose Bowl debacle of 1961.

Ohio State's Athletic Ticket Office reported that student ticket sales had fallen to a ten-year low; 88 percent of all eligible students had bought tickets in 1957, but in 1967, only 55 percent did so.

After a particularly ignominious 41–6 defeat at the hands of Purdue, rumors of a player rebellion against Hayes's outdated approach to the game spread. Longtime Buckeye boosters, including local television sportscaster Jimmy Crum, openly questioned the coach and team's motivation. *Sports Illustrated*, always quick to point out the flaws in Ohio State's programs, speculated Buckeye football was "dead." The *Lantern* agreed, piling on in an October 12 editorial, "Football dominance is over….Times are changing. Students just don't have the time to become enthusiastic about football. The *Lantern* doesn't say that this is good or bad. We're saying that it has happened."

Hayes did manage to rally his troops to finish the Big Ten season with a 5–2 record, including a 24–14 win over Michigan. He sounded optimistic when touting the strength of the returning freshmen for the next year. Some fans got excited, but skeptics took a wait-and-see approach.

Basketball: Is the Magic Back?

After a string of disappointing seasons, Fred Taylor's minions finally gave fans something to cheer about. Led by six-foot-seven-inch-tall center Bill Hosket, the team captured the Big Ten title and established a conference record for field goal percentage. They upset the heavily favored Kentucky to earn a trip to the Final Four in Los Angeles, where they were knocked out by North Carolina in the first round (80–66) but came back and beat heavily favored Houston (89–85) to clinch third place.

PLACES

University Hall Bites the Dust

Venerable University Hall, which was ninety-four years old in 1968, finally began its death spiral. Students had been complaining about the safety of the building since at least the late 1940s. In 1966, an engineering study concluded that University Hall was beyond rehabilitation. The following year, an eight-hundred-pound piece of sandstone fell from the facing; fortunately, no one was hurt. Maintenance people rushed to shore up a sagging third floor, and in classic Ohio State fashion, people argued back and forth for the next three years about what to do with the building. University Hall was finally torn down in 1971, and it was replaced with a near replica six years later.

Bookstore Backlash

The campus area's three bookstores were a source of both continuity and frustration for legions of students. Long's had been around the longest; it was started by student Frank C. Long in 1902 and had been at its prime location at the corner of Fifteenth and High Streets since 1909. The University Bookstore was opened in Lord Hall in 1926, and it was moved to the basement of Derby Hall a year later. The Student Book Exchange, located one block south of Long's at 1806 North High Street, was opened in May 1953.

The bookstore rush was a familiar sight at the beginning of the fall quarter. *Courtesy of the* Makio.

Bookstores were always a target for students who were unhappy about the price of textbooks. One Long's manager told the *Lantern*, "I don't know why books are made the whipping boy. Inflation on books is less than that on other items. There were no objections when the price of beer and cigarettes recently advanced." Faced with narrow margins on books, all three stores sought to peddle other items with higher margins, which critics also attacked. Despite all this, they remained remarkably viable and even survived an attempt to establish a co-op bookstore in the 1970s.

Changing times finally caught up with the bookstores in the new millennium. Ohio State contracted out its bookstore to Barnes and Noble in 2005, and it was moved to the Gateway development on the south end of campus. Long's was sold to Gateway in 2000 and closed in 2005; its distinctive sign was moved to the new Barnes and Noble. The Student Book Exchange was closed in 2017.

New Freedoms, New Players

Harrison House, a privately owned 520-student coed apartment building on West Lane Avenue, opened in the fall of 1967. It symbolized the growth of off-campus rental space, which was built to meet students' increasing demand for the freedom of apartment living.

Harrison House, a privately owned coed apartment building, was opened on West Lane Avenue in the fall of 1967. *Courtesy of the* Lantern.

Other new establishments that year included a new chain restaurant, the International House of Pancakes (IHOP), which offered meals until 2:00 a.m. on weekends under its blue-tiled roof at the corner of High and Norwich Streets. The campus gained its first Mexican restaurant, Taco Village, at Hunter and Eleventh Avenues, and it gained a new poster store, Postermint, at 8 East Thirteenth Avenue. The trend toward spacious nightclubs featuring live entertainment continued with the opening of Peabody's Warehouse across from the Ohio Union at 1716 North High Street, where the Sacred Mushroom used to be, and the Draught House, which was further north, at 2650 North High Street.

FASHION

The Year of You

"This is the year when anything that looks good on you is 'in,'" the *Lantern* declared in its 1967–68 fashion preview. Indeed, "doing your own thing" seemed to be the watchword: miniskirts, micro-minis, midis, maxis, culottes and even pants were in for women. Plaids and paisleys were big for both women and men, as were flower patterns. Wire-rimmed glasses became fashionable thanks to the Beatle John Lennon.

It was a tough time for campus barbershops, which suffered as a result of the trend toward longer hair on men. William Martin of Martin's Barber Shop at 1961 North High explained, "It really hurts business when a man who used to come in every two or three weeks now comes in every two months." William Marple of Marple's Barber Shop at 1930 North High told the *Lantern* that he had cut back his chairs from five to three. He said, "And the way things are today, you have to look twice to see if you're trimming a boy or a girl."

Eyewear, including wire-rimmed glasses (*left*) and aviator-type sunglasses (*right*) were part of the 1968 fashion milieu. *Courtesy of the* Lantern.

This happening couple (*left*) rates a fashion plate 1968 award. Note the shoes with no socks on the man. Blue jeans had replaced white Levi's. Shirts with no collar were trendy, as were facial hair and wire-rimmed glasses. The woman sported a short flowered dress and a beaded necklace. Her hair was little shorter than the norm, but it was stylishly cut. This Nehru jacket (*right*) represented one of the more questionable fads of the late 1960s. *Courtesy of the* Makio.

9

DAWN OF THE AGE OF AQUARIUS

1968-69

The moon was in the seventh house. Jupiter was aligned with Mars. Peace guided the planets, and love steered the stars. And so it went in the signature song from *Hair*, the rock musical that captured the spirt of the late 1960s. On the Ohio State campus, the dawn of the Age of Aquarius was a conflicted mix of the old and the new, the traditional and the edgy.

ATHLETICS

Woody's Revenge

Woody Hayes had ended the 1967 football season by touting his returning freshmen for 1968. Fans even began to whisper about a possible Rose Bowl at the end of the rainbow. Opposing coaches took notice, but they were more guarded. They rated Ohio State eleventh in the Associated Press Coaches' Poll as the season opened. The Buckeyes proceeded to win their first games against two nonconference opponents, Southern Methodist University and the University of Oregon, with a combined score of 56–20. The returning freshmen, already dubbed the Super Sophomores, included the likes of quarterback Rex Kern, defensive backs Mike Sensibaugh and Jack Tatum and middle linebacker Jim Stillwagon. Nevertheless,

Even at the dawn of the Age of Aquarius, a storied tradition captured the hearts and minds of Buckeyes everywhere. *Courtesy of the* Makio.

critics expected them to be humbled when mighty Purdue came to town on October 12. The Boilermakers roared into Columbus ranked no. 1 in the country, and they sported an offensive juggernaut that averaged an incredible forty-one points per game. But the Super Sophomores shut them down 13–0 before a record crowd of 84,838. It was the first time Purdue had been shut out in twenty-eight games.

The Buckeyes went on to win their next five games, making their record 8–0, and they outscored their opponents 177–100, raising their poll ranking to no. 2. They already had a Rose Bowl contract, and unlike in 1961, no one was going to say no. All that stood in the Buckeyes' way was the University of Michigan, whose no. 4–ranked Wolverines boasted an 8–1 record.

Left: Fullback Jim Otis launched off the shoulders of Michigan linebacker Phil Seymour (91) to score six points on November 23. *Courtesy of the* Makio. *Right*: Down came the goalposts after a decisive 50–14 win over Michigan, which guaranteed the Buckeyes a place at the Rose Bowl. *Courtesy of the* Lantern.

Over sixty media outlets crammed into the press box and onto the sidelines of Ohio Stadium on Saturday, November 23, 1968, to cover a game that was also being broadcast overseas via Armed Forces Radio. More than 85,370 fans filled the Horseshoe; it was the third record-breaking crowd of the year. Some who couldn't get into the game were lucky enough to receive a weak UHF signal from WOSU-TV (there was no cable in those days). Michigan's governor George Romney had tried unsuccessfully to get ABC to pick up the game, so WOSU agreed to run a closed-circuit link to Ann Arbor. Michigan fans need not have bothered. Woody's fired-up Buckeyes rolled over the weak Wolverines 50–14. Delirious fans began celebrating immediately (see "Party Time" below).

As clean-up began on Sunday morning, the campus was already looking ahead to January 1. The Buckeyes faced the no. 2–ranked University of Southern California (USC), which had a high-powered offense led by Trojan running back and Heisman Trophy winner O.J. Simpson. It marked the first time in the pre–Bowl Championship Series days that two unbeaten teams met in the nation's premier postseason contest. The crowd of 105,000 included at least 15,000 Ohio State fans; among them, were 5,000 students who had paid $4.50 each for tickets. Numerous luminaries attended as well, including president-elect Richard M. Nixon and his wife, Pat, who spent each half of the game on a different sideline. Millions more watched in living color on NBC.

The Trojans scored first, but it didn't matter. The Super Sophomores forced five USC turnovers, including two by Simpson, and Ohio State

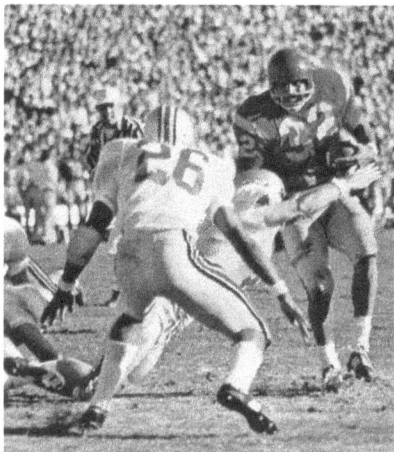

Left: Ohio State defensive back Tim Anderson (26) prepares to stuff O.J. Simpson (32) at the Rose Bowl. *Courtesy of the* Makio. *Right*: A crowd of two thousand people braved the fifteen-degree weather to welcome the Buckeyes home at Port Columbus on January 3, 1969. *Courtesy of the* Lantern.

triumphed, 27–16. Now, the Buckeyes truly were no. 1. Woody Hayes was named Coach of the Year and then headed off for his third Vietnam tour to share Rose Bowl highlights with the troops.

PARTY TIME

High Street and Beyond

Events celebrating Ohio State's victorious football season dominated the fall quarter's social calendar. The celebrations began after the October 12 victory over heavily favored Purdue. Four thousand enthused fans celebrated at Fifteenth and High Streets in what might be described as a giant party. Even Columbus police got into the spirit; ten cruisers escorted 350 students who marched through downtown and back without incident.

The November 23 victory over Michigan generated an even bigger celebration. The steel goalposts came down for the first time in ten years, and a boisterous band of students carried them down High Street, chanting, "We're no. 1! We're no. 1!" It was one of several parades that evening, including a procession of six thousand students led by the marching band.

Ohio State students celebrate after the victory over Michigan on November 23. *Courtesy of the* Makio.

As *Lantern* reporter Kay Burtscher wrote, "Thousands of Ohio State students threw a nine-hour party...from the campus to downtown Columbus." City police remained low-key as they escorted marchers, cordoned off High Street from Eleventh to Lane Avenues as a party zone and ignored open containers. Many students expressed their appreciation by bedecking officers with roses. By midnight, things got a little ragged. Police had to arrest twelve students, and a cold drizzle took care of the rest. The party broke up around 1:30 a.m. It left in its wake a significant amount of property damage. Police "just didn't expect a celebration of this magnitude," one officer confessed.

Energetic students found other outlets as well—some traditional, some not. Although they had failed in their previous efforts to allow beer in the living units, beer in the student union turned out to be a winner. The Ohio Union Tavern sold 45 kegs, or 698 gallons, of 3.2 percent beer during the first week of fall quarter. Crowds as large as three thousand overflowed into the cafeteria and the Terrace dining room.

Theme parties, which had begun to wane, staged a resurgence during Greek Week. Fraternities and sororities banded together to throw parties based on the classics of literature. Phi Gamma Delta, Delta Upsilon, Chi Phi and Alpha Epsilon Pi invited guests to the Fiji house to "follow the Yellow Brick Road" as part of a Wizard of Oz theme. Partygoers could walk through a tornado-whipped village and visit a Kansas cornfield and a witch's castle.

Beer came to the Ohio Union. Senior Bruce Barber drew the first pitcher for eager junior Vine Hill. *Courtesy of the* Lantern.

Left: Freshman Merry Stinson ended up on the short end of a north campus water fight. "We didn't have any backup strength," she complained. *Courtesy of the* Lantern. *Right*: Torrential rains provided the stimulus for a May Week mud fight on the Oval. *Courtesy of the* Makio.

Theta Chi, Alpha Tau Omega, Phi Kappa Sigma and Kappa Alpha Theta hosted guests at a Dante's Inferno party at the Theta Chi house, where they had to cross a river of blood, walk through a tunnel of horrors and witness scenes from Hell.

Flash crowds were the order of the day in the spring. They included an all–north campus water fight on April 8 and a mud battle on the Oval a month later.

Where the Boys Are

A spring break party trip to Florida beaches was a college ritual throughout the 1960s. It even produced a celebratory Hollywood movie (1961's *Where the Boys Are*). In March 1969, the *Lantern* documented the extent of this migration. More than five thousand Ohio State students, about one-eighth of the student body, made the trek that year to enjoy a week of sun and partying. The nine-hundred-plus-mile trip typically took twenty-two to twenty-six hours to complete one way. When split among four students, the costs came to only $30 to $35 for car rental and gas for the round trip. A round trip to Fort Lauderdale on a Greyhound bus cost $77.40 and took thirty-six hours each way.

For those with the money to fly, Delta and Eastern Airlines offered flights from Port Columbus. Flying Delta to Daytona cost $132 round trip (or about $900 in today's prices), but it only cost $47 for the special youth rate for those under twenty-one. The cost of an Eastern flight to Fort Lauderdale was similar. Students could also take a package tour. No matter how they got there, spring break in Florida was a chance for students to party without restraint.

Spring Recess
March 17-24, 1969

MIAMI BEACH
8 days $168

ROUND TRIP TRANSPORTATION via chartered jet between Columbus and Miami
ROUND TRIP TRANSFERS between Miami International Airport and the Nautilus
HOTEL ACCOMMODATIONS at the Nautilus for 8 days
WEENIE ROAST
FREE CHAISE LOUNGES
SURFING (If you know how)
ENTERTAINMENT Nightly
RADIO and TV in every room
HOTEL TAXES
GRATUITIES TO Bellboys and Maids
TRAVEL WALLET and BAGGAGE TAGS
Also available: Jet fare only
For information call:
Mr. Howard Hoffman 299-6671, 299-6777
Mr. Gary Sloan 291-5304
1968 Indianola Avenue
Columbus, Ohio 43201
Arrangements by LIBERTY TRAVEL GROUPS

Spring break attracted entrepreneurs who offered package deals like this one in a January 1969 advertisement. *Courtesy of the* Lantern.

A Legend Is Born

That summer, some Ohio State students participated in the ultimate flash crowd of the 1960s: Woodstock. Nearly half a million young people gathered in upstate New York in mid-August 1969 for "three days of peace and music," celebrating the counterculture. *Lantern* reporter Tom Burroughs was one such young person. He wrote, "After the shock of the fantastic size wore off, it didn't take long for the people to realize that the occasion was something not of the ordinary…and the people were beginning it together, and would stay together. Together became not just a word but a way of living."

Woodstock participants and counterculture supporters believed they were accomplishing something larger than just entertaining themselves. They overcame rain, mud and lack of food, water and sanitary facilities by sharing as a community, without force and without violence. They called the spirit Woodstock Nation, and although it was very real during those three days, its transference to the rest of society was not in the cards.

This advertisement ran in the *Lantern* on August 7, 1969. The three-day ticket price of $18 translates to more than $120 today. *Courtesy of the* Lantern.

TRADITIONS

Under Siege

While rumors of the demise of Ohio State football turned out to be wildly premature, the Age of Aquarius did not dawn well for other traditions.

Homecoming Calamity

With the theme of Colonial Calamity, Homecoming offered a spirited pep rally on Friday night and a victorious Homecoming game on Saturday. Sophomore Suzi Young was crowned Homecoming Queen in a scandal-free election, and the float contest avoided drenching rain. However, other signs of discontent manifested themselves.

Black students, who had felt left out of Homecoming in the past, split off to run their own queen contest and chose sophomore Leola Johnson from seventeen finalists at an Ohio Union dance on Saturday. More than 1,500 attended the dance, which was sponsored by black fraternity Alpha Phi Alpha.

The *Lantern* said that the Homecoming concert choice of pianist Peter Nero and comedian Frank Welker was more appropriate for the class of 1956. Students agreed, and concert attendance fell off. "Colonial Calamity turned into a financial calamity," crowed the *Lantern*.

Pick on Greeks Week

By traditional measures, Greek Week was again a success: five hundred pints of blood were donated, $6,200 was raised for the Heart Fund and—in a new touch—105 underprivileged children were treated to dinner. Peter, Paul and Mary entertained in St. John Arena. But the Greek system itself continued to show signs of strain. According to the Alumni Interfraternity Council, thirty of the forty-four fraternities at Ohio State were rated as being in critical or very critical shape financially due to the rising costs and declining memberships. One fraternity, Alpha Kappa Lambda, had already folded. And the *Lantern* went after both fraternities and sororities for their lack of diversity and what it called "perpetuation of the prejudice brought from the suburbs."

Golddiggers Bites the Dust

The Women's Self Government Association finally gave up on the Golddiggers Dance, as it fell victim to decreasing interest. The event was replaced with the election of a May King as part of the May Week festivities.

May Week: Somebody Up There Hates Us

May Week planners moved all outdoor events to the intramural fields by the hospitals to provide more room for more activities, including a frisbee contest. But the weather gods did not cooperate, and things were rained out for the second year in a row. Ten thousand people did attend the indoor carnival.

Students elected their first black May Queen, independent freshman Andrea Walker, and their first May King, senior varsity linebacker Mark Stier of Kappa Sigma fraternity. For the third year in a row, ROTC activities were the target of demonstrators. Because of the weather, the ROTC ceremony had been moved to Mershon Auditorium, where thirty state highway patrolmen in riot gear kept things in hand. Instead, protestors and supporters traded insults and fisticuffs outside the auditorium.

The May Week initiation of members in chimes honorary before the rains came was a tradition that endured. *Courtesy of the* Makio.

New Traditions Emerge

While old traditions wavered, some newer activities picked up momentum. The tenth-annual Sigma Chi Derby Day, which included sorority women chasing fraternity men to snatch derbies off their heads, benefited from good April weather and growing enthusiasm. The fourth-annual WSGA Bridal Fair in the Ohio Union drew two thousand prospective brides to view gowns and other accoutrements.

After years of feeling marginalized on a predominantly white campus, African American students began to take things into their own hands with the first black Homecoming event and other activities. In February, the

Above: A newer tradition. Sigma Chi Derby Day (*left*) attracted the playful and an older tradition, the WSGA Bridal Fair (*right*) attracted the hopeful. *Courtesy of the* Makio

Left: Black History Week in February included a fashion show. *Courtesy of the* Makio.

Black Student Union and the university cosponsored Black History Week at the Ohio Union. Events ranged from a fashion show to an exhibition by black artists, including Earl Scarborough, who coined the phrase "black is beautiful."

SHOWTIME

Goodbye Columbus

A connection to Columbus and Ohio State was embedded in the 1969 movie *Goodbye Columbus*. Based on the Philip Roth novel of the same name, the film featured Ali McGraw and Richard Benjamin in their debut roles. One character was a former Buckeye basketball player who hung around the house playing recordings of the Ohio State Marching Band. The *Lantern* gave the movie credit as "marvelous entertainment" but said it "fails as art." Audiences loved it anyway, making it one of the top movies of the year. Others that appealed to college students included several that became classics of the decade: *Midnight Cowboy*, *Romeo and Juliet*, *Bob and Carol and Ted and Alice*, and *Easy Rider.*

Arena Rock

Ohio State led the trend of providing larger venues for popular music by opening St. John Arena to Simon and Garfunkel on October 5 and Peter, Paul and Mary, who were returning to campus yet again, on February 7. Mershon Auditorium chipped in to host Smokey Robinson on January 24

Ravi Shankar and his psychedelic sitar at Mershon. *Courtesy of the* Makio.

and Ravi Shankar on April 23. Local nightclubs showed they were a growing force. The Bistro led the way with Linda Ronstadt and the Stone Poneys for a week in October. Others included the American Breed and Mitch Ryder at the Draught House, the Peppermint Rainbow at the Sugar Shack and Spencer Davis at the Castle.

I Am Curious, Porno

The line from the World Theater's box office snaked north along High Street and around the corner in what would turn out to be the largest cinema event of the decade. Midnight on Thursday was not usually the prime time to release a new movie, but on July 3, 1969, that logic went up in smoke. What the crowd had turned out for was already known to be no masterpiece in terms of writing, directing, acting or photography. But those in line hoped to be the first in town to see the Swedish-made *I Am Curious (Yellow)*. The controversial film purported to be a documentary about making a porno flick, and in doing so, it pushed the boundaries of what was acceptable in terms of graphic depictions of sex on the big screen.

Columbus was still a conservative town; the *Dispatch* refused to review the film and others like it, and it would not accept paid advertising for them. Just a little more than two years earlier, the ever-vigilant Columbus police vice squad had seized the controversial film *I, a Woman* and tossed the manager of the World Theater into the slammer. A lot had changed since then; the Broadway show *Hair* even included nudity on stage. But no one knew what to expect that night in Columbus.

The *Lantern* dispatched two reporters to cover the movie and the surrounding hoopla. Regular film critic Mike Clark described the entire event as a "circus," but he was more forgiving about the movie. "Some of the scenes were good. Even more were dull. Even more were graphic," he wrote. "Who could complain?" Clark pointed out that he managed to sit through the whole movie, which is more than he could say for *The Maltese Bippy*, which drove him out of the theater after only twenty-five minutes.

Lantern staff writer David Milenthal found a number of things to complain about under the headline "Swedish Sex Movie Pleases Area Voyeurs." For example, he found the lead character's forty-five minutes of interviews with people about Swedish politics was more than he could stand. "If there is any more resemblance of meaning to the film," he concluded, "I don't know what it could be. The film's merit is in its sexual thought, and its sexual

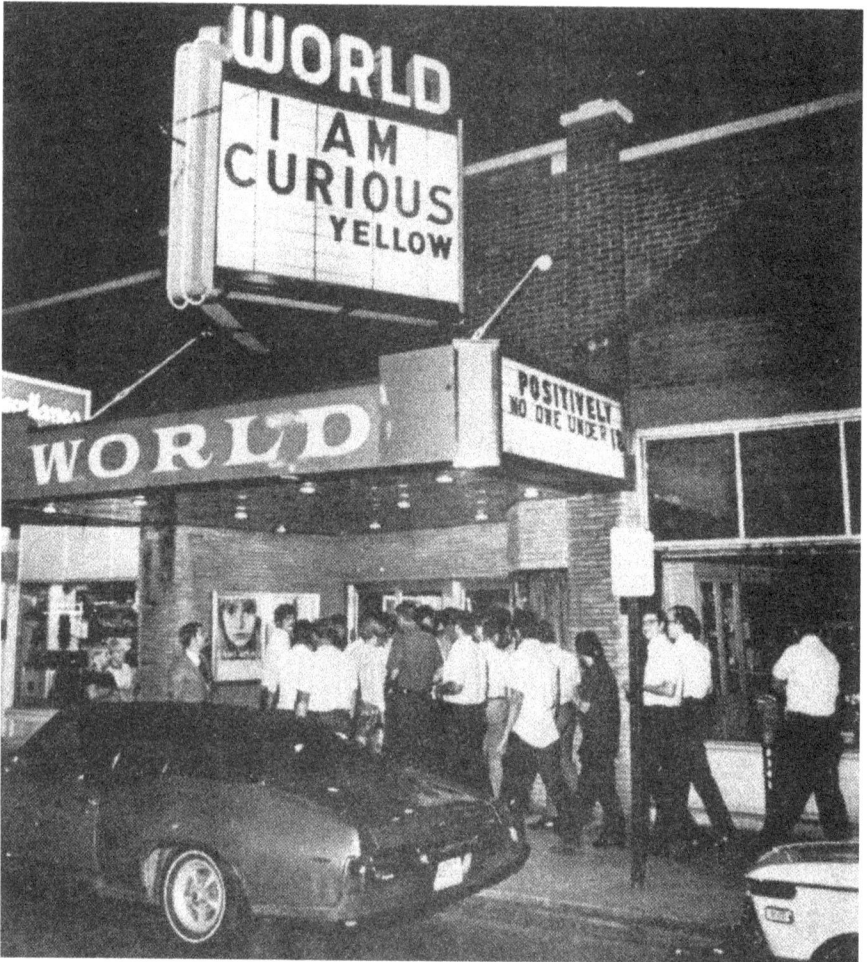

The curious lined up to see *I Am Curious (Yellow)* at the World Theater in July. *Courtesy of the* Lantern.

thought is in the gutter. I must agree with a vice squadman who said after seeing the film, 'If people are willing to pay to see this kind of trash, then let them go.' It is sad, of course, to think that long lines extend from the theatre, as people anxiously await their mental orgasms. But wait—why did I stand in line?" Milenthal recovered enough from the experience to graduate and start one of central Ohio's most successful public relations firms.

The vice squad did not close down the World Theater, which made plenty of money on *I Am Curious (Yellow)*, and a flood of more explicit sex films had just begun.

PLACES

Haight on High Street

When the counterculture first pierced the national consciousness in the middle of 1967, both the Ohio State campus and the surrounding community reacted with skepticism and, in some cases, downright hostility (see "Counterculture: Not so Fast" in chapter seven). To the horror of their elders, by the middle of 1969, young people at Ohio State and elsewhere had fully embraced the counterculture, leaving behind the accepted values of suburban and small-town America that they had grown up with.

The counterculture's symbolic epicenter at Ohio State revolved around an eclectic collection of small shops, including Charlie's Guitar and Venus Coffee House, that filled a one-block stretch of commercial real estate on Thirteenth Avenue, just across High Street from the Ohio Union. Known as Pearl Alley, it became the preferred gathering place for the growing numbers of students and the many former students living in nearby apartments and rooming houses. They shared a lifestyle that differed from the traditional norms in its attitudes toward appearance, music, sex

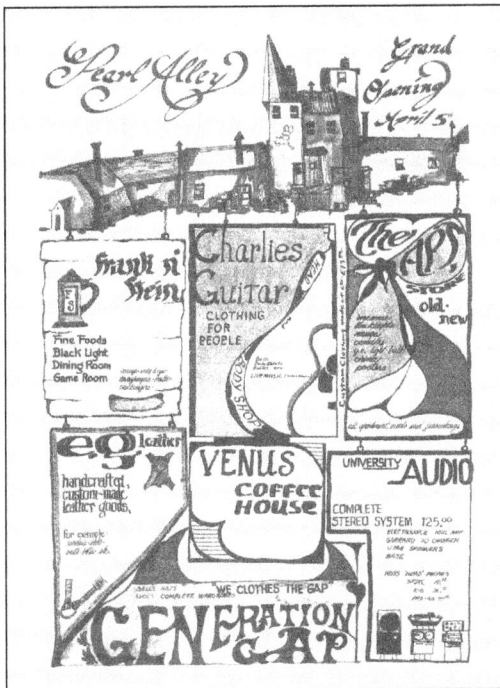

This advertisement from April 1969 announced the opening of Pearl Alley, which became the epicenter of the counterculture at Ohio State. *Courtesy of the* Lantern.

and drugs. As one shop owner put it, "We just wanted to live the way we wanted to, with no outside intervention." That view was not shared by law enforcement, and Pearl Alley became another flashpoint in the deteriorating relationship between the university's youth culture and the Columbus police.

The 1968–69 school year also witnessed the opening of a big-box nightclub, the two-story Castle at 1778 North High Street, across from the Ohio Union; another fast-food franchise, Arthur Treacher's Fish and Chips at 2183 North High Street; and another head shop, Miscellanea at 2157 North High Street, next to the World Theater.

Parking: Damn the Torpedoes

Despite the opening of a second garage next to the Ohio Union, parking continued to frustrate students. The *Lantern* called it a "vicious circle" while chastising university officials for not doing enough to ease the pain.

The *Lantern* decided to follow sophomore Chris Walker through her parking travails. *Left*: she demonstrates the saying "if it feels good, do it" by tearing up her fifth parking ticket. *Right*: she learns the meaning of the phrase "decisions have consequences." She got her car back from the impound lot after being forced to grovel to the parking gods and pay her outstanding tickets, plus a ten-dollar impoundment fee. *Courtesy of the* Lantern.

FASHION

Long Hair and Bell-Bottoms

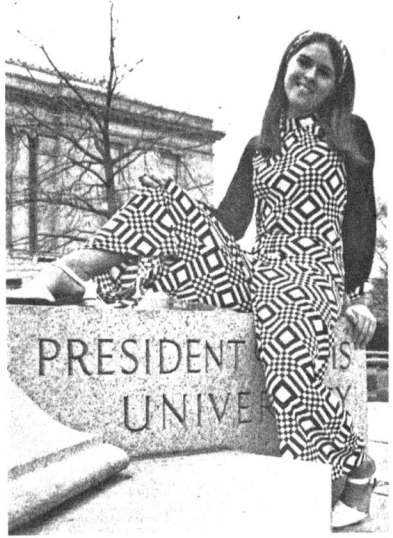

Right: Fashion plate 1969: junior Samantha Hofer modeled a stylish pantsuit with a pattern resembling a computer chip. Note the matching hairband. *Courtesy of the* Lantern.

Below: Fashion Plate II: this content couple sported a number of popular unisex style trends, including blue jeans and plenty of hair, but they had no socks and no four on the floor. *Courtesy of the* Makio.

10

START THE REVOLUTION

1969-70

or three years, officials had been planning to make 1970 a yearlong celebration of Ohio State's one hundredth anniversary. Instead, they had to shut the university down when student protests became unmanageable. Ohio State would never face student unrest of this magnitude again; it left a legacy of fundamental changes in the way the university operates. The decade also left in its wake other elements of a cultural revolution that are still very much with us today.

ATHLETICS

Wolverines' Revenge

Expectations soared as the 1969 football season opened. After all, the Buckeyes had been the country's top team the year before, and the core of the Super Sophomores were returning as Super Juniors. The experts agreed, and they ranked Ohio State no. 1 in all the preseason polls. Rumors about a cutback in the student ticket allocation sparked panic buying. On the first day tickets were offered, four thousand students waited for six hours in a line that stretched from St. John Arena to the Lane Avenue Bridge. The rumor turned out be false. All the student tickets were eventually sold, as were all the others.

Students support the call for a strike against the university in the spring of 1970. *Courtesy of the* Makio.

Results of the first eight games of the season justified the high expectations. The Buckeyes outscored their overmatched opponents with a combined score of 371–69, or an average of 46–9 per game. Not only did the Buckeyes win every game, they never trailed. The only cloud on the horizon was the NCAA rule that did not allow a team to play in the Rose Bowl two years in a row. Fans wanted Ohio State to appeal, but university officials knew that would be hopeless. So, speculation began as to who might be a worthy opponent in one of the other bowl games to establish the team's second straight national championship.

Of course, the Buckeyes still had to win their remaining game against Michigan in Ann Arbor. The Wolverines were not pushovers; they held a 6–2 record, which was good for twelfth place in the national polls. However, Ohio State was clearly favored with eight All-Americans on its roster and a seventeen-point spread. Michigan's rookie coach Bo Schembechler did all he could to gin up his underdogs for the game. He posted a big "50" in the locker room to represent the number of points the team had let Ohio State score against them the year before. He also told his players that they would not get to the Rose Bowl through the back door; in other words, they had to beat Ohio State or stay home.

Twenty-three thousand enthusiastic fans made the trip from Columbus to be part of a record crowd of 103,508 in the Big House on November 22. ABC-TV broadcast the matchup live as the game of the week, but ugly is what people witnessed. Woody's sure-handed team, which had averaged more than forty points per game, only scored six points while committing six interceptions and a fumble on the way to a humiliating 24–12 defeat. ABC's play-by-play announcer exclaimed, "There it is! What has to be the upset of the century!" Six months later, still shell-shocked Ohio State fans received a small measure of consolation when ABC Sports named the 1968 team the decade's best, eclipsing the 1961 Alabama Crimson Tide and the 1962 University of Southern California Trojans.

The basketball Buckeyes also generated high expectations. With All-American center Dave Sorenson and power forward Jim Cleamons, both seniors, this was the team's big chance. They did establish an all-time NCAA shooting record, but they finished with a disappointing 17–7 record, which was only good for third place in the Big Ten.

Disappointment showed clearly on the face of sophomore cheerleader Sally Eickholt (*left*), while two unidentified fans lingered in agony in the Big House after the game (*right*). *Courtesy of the* Makio.

TRADITIONS

Homecoming Gets the Beat

The Traditions Board finally got the message after nearly half a decade of ignoring students' mounting dissatisfaction with Homecoming entertainment. Enter Blood, Sweat and Tears, the nine-man rock-jazz fusion band that had charted three singles and its debut album in the national top ten over the preceding twelve months. The group sold out all eleven thousand seats in St. John Arena for their concert on October 24, and it delivered a well-received performance. The Homecoming Queen election was not tainted by scandal, the Buckeyes pulled off a thrashing of Illinois in the Horseshoe (41–0), the weather was good for the parade and floats and Disneyland OSU turned out to be a good show. Even the *Lantern* admitted the event was a success. Homecoming would continue as a great tradition into the next millennium.

You came and you took control. Lead singer David Clayton Thomas whooped it up for an appreciative audience after the traditions board finally got with it and invited Blood, Sweat and Tears to Homecoming in 1969. *Courtesy of the* Makio.

Greek Week Rebrands

Stung by growing criticism of irrelevance, Ohio State's fraternities and sororities worked to improve their images by focusing on service during Greek Week. "We want to show independents [that] Greeks are no longer part of the stereotyped 50s of booze and football," chair Geoff Webster told the *Lantern*. Greek Week events included raising $5,100 for the Heart Fund and dispatching six hundred volunteers into the community for service projects.

Nevertheless, the Greek system continued to struggle to overcome accusations of being outdated and segregated. In November, the *Lantern* reported incidences of illegal hazing. An attempt to demonstrate solidarity between black and white Greeks with a February exchange dinner blew up when Ben Parks, president of black fraternity Omega Psi Phi, was accosted by two guard dogs when he went to visit a white fraternity house to plan the event. The event was subsequently called off.

A service-oriented Greek Week. *Left to right*: freshman Arlene Freeman, sophomore Jim Williams and juniors Mark Sheehan and Jim Wayman treated Mark Falm, a student at the Ohio State School for the Blind, to a pony ride at the Phi Delta Theta house. *Courtesy of the* Lantern.

Even Sigma Chi Derby Day turned into a controversy. Three sororities dropped out of the tenth-annual event in April because they believed that the signature activity—women chasing men to capture their derbies—was "unnecessarily rough and humiliating." Sigma Chi agreed to make some changes, and Derby Day exists today as a charity fundraiser.

The Greek system at Ohio State was never able to restore itself to the dominance it had in the early 1960s, but membership stabilized at about three thousand members, and Greek Week continued as a service-oriented tradition.

Bridal Fair Expires While Black History Thrives

The fifth-annual Women's Self Government Association (WSGA) Bridal Fair went on as scheduled on February 5, but the event's days were numbered. By 1973, declining attendance and growing criticism by women's groups caused the sponsors to cancel it for good. WSGA put itself out of business in 1975.

A celebration of African American musical heritage during Black Culture Week. *Courtesy of the* Makio.

The third-annual Black History Week was celebrated in February. Black Culture Week had debuted in November and was sponsored by the Kennedy-King Action Corps, the Ohio State chapter of the NAACP, the Black Arts Society, the South Campus Student Association and Ohio Union Activities. The purpose of the event, according to Paula Dickson, assistant director of Ohio Union Activities, was to make people aware that "worthwhile things are being done in the arts by black people." Black Culture Week eventually morphed into the African American Heritage Festival in April, and Black History Week became Black History Month.

May Week: Sorry 'Bout That

The Traditions Board had planned the biggest and best May Week ever in 1970 under the awkward banner of Yesterday, YesterMay, Yes-Today! Instead, Ohio State officials canceled all events and dedicated May 6 as a day of reflection in the wake of the killings of four students on the Kent State campus by Ohio National Guardsmen two days earlier. The university then shut down for two weeks as safety concerns overwhelmed available resources.

May Week organizers were left holding the bag with some interesting problems, including 9,500 frozen chicken halves that had been procured for the annual supper. They were sold to the university food service, which kept them frozen until they were served in the dining halls when students returned later that month. The May Week pop concert, which was scheduled for May 8 and featured guitarist Mason Williams, was canceled under the act of God clause in the contract and tickets were refunded. The May Queen crowning also had to be canceled, which left ten contestants with expensive ensembles they had paid for themselves and nothing to show for it. The ROTC ceremonies had already been moved off the Oval, but they still attracted protestors on May 4.

May Week returned to the Oval the following year, but by the mid-1970s, it had fallen victim to student apathy. Attempts were made to revive it after that, but it was put out of business for good when the first week of May became finals week after the university switched to a semester schedule in 2013. The ROTC ceremonies did not return until 2008. The ROTC program survives, but it is much smaller than it was in its heyday in the mid-1960s.

Makio Struggles

The slimmed-down 1969 *Makio* sold 4,600 copies, allowing that tradition to continue—but not without a struggle. Sales declined in the 1970s, and the yearbook did not appear at all in 1979; it disappeared again between 1995 and 2000. It has since resumed publication, but in some years, it has sold as little as three hundred copies. On the other hand, *Dates and Data*, the smaller, cheaper and more-topical appointment book published by Ohio Union Activities, has continued to thrive without interruption.

SHOWTIME

Get It On

Homecoming headliners Blood, Sweat and Tears led a robust roster of pop music icons as the university finally shook off its infatuation with the had-beens of the late 1950s and early 1960s. Sam and Dave, accompanied by a fourteen-piece soul band, kicked off fall quarter with a lively concert before a full house at the Ohio Union on October 2. Sponsored by a group of black students called Buckeye Brothers, Sam and Dave owned the classic song "Soul Man" and reportedly served as inspiration for both Otis Day and the Knights of *Animal House* fame and John Belushi and Dan Aykroyd's Blues Brothers on *Saturday Night Live*.

Two weeks later, the Buckeye Brothers joined forces with Sigma Chi fraternity to present the Ohio Players, an eight-man soul-funk band from Dayton. Relatively unknown at the time, the Ohio Players went on to become major recording stars of the mid-1970s.

The Ohio Staters jumped in next by bringing The Association back to St. John Arena in November. The group had offered a less-than-inspired performance at Mershon Auditorium in 1967 (see chapter seven), but this time, they were more than up to the task, and no one walked out. Aided by a $45,000 sound system they brought with them, the group was in top form; *Lantern* reviewer Jody Ross gushed that they were "even better than the records." They played "Goodbye Columbus" for the local crowd, but the high point of the concert came when they performed "Enter the Young," which they dedicated to participants in the Vietnam Moratorium protest march the next day.

Fall quarter also witnessed Cleveland's James Gang, which featured former Ohio State student Jimmy Fox, and a light show at the World Theater on October 17; the Box Tops performed at the Castle on October 20. Mershon hosted the unusual pairing of comedian and impressionist David Frye and Motown star Little Anthony on January 23. The combination drew a sparse crowd, but once Frye got into his repertoire of an overly folksy Lyndon Johnson, a pompous William Buckley and a paranoid Richard Nixon, the audience roared with laughter.

Greek Week brought Gary Puckett and the Union Gap to Mershon on February 17 to perform the group's hit singles as well as some jazz and blues. April brought West Coast blues rockers Pacific Gas and Electric to the Draught House, and it brought arm-waver Joe Cocker to the Ohio Theatre downtown. Veterans Memorial chipped in with English guitar-wreckers the Who in November, the Band in December, Three Dog Night in February, blue-eyed folksinger Judy Collins in March and jazz fusion ensemble Chicago in May.

The spring concert season on campus ended with Ohio Staters sponsoring the highly popular Fifth Dimension in St. John Arena in April.

Home-Grown

Members of the Ohio State family produced some innovative and, in a few cases, new or controversial events of their own. Nudity on the stage was big in New York City in 1969 (in shows like *Hair* and *Oh! Calcutta!*), and while Columbus wasn't ready to go that far, it did inch closer. In November, the University Theatre presented *Lysistrata*, an ancient and edgy Greek comedy that *Lantern* critic Bruce Vilanch dubbed "Aristophanes meets Barbarella." It featured foam-rubber phalluses on the male actors and what Vilanch described as "some of the sexiest, sleekest, space-aged and spaced-out chorus girls imaginable." *Lysistrata* quickly earned the nickname "I Am Curious: Greek," which was a play off the title of the Swedish sex movie *I Am Curious (Yellow)*, which had played at the World Theater earlier in the year.

The Ohio Union's Creative Arts Festival was not as controversial, but it did establish a new campus tradition. The festival included an all-day rock concert on the Oval on Sunday, April 26, and it was a big success. It became an annual event and is still going strong today.

The University
Theatre
production of
Lysistrata invited
comparisons
to *I Am Curious
(Yellow)*. *Courtesy of
the* Makio.

The new Creative Arts Festival included a rock concert on the Oval. The now-annual event remains popular nearly fifty years later. *Courtesy of the* Lantern.

The Movies and the Message

In a January 1970 opinion piece, *Lantern* columnist Gail Bryce hailed a new era in cinema. "A bloodless revolution is taking place," she wrote, "and the good guys are winning. The young are snatching the movie cameras from the hands of their elders and are breaking new ground.... If the current trends continue, I predict that movies in the 1970's will be the dominant form of communication, the main mode of transmitting new ideas, the major influence of life-styles." As with much of the inflated rhetoric of the time, events didn't unfold quite as dramatically as Bryce said they would, and the establishment ended up in firm control. Nevertheless, Hollywood did recognize the need to cater to the growing market power of baby boomers, and it turned to younger producers and directors to lead the way.

One of the decade's films produced by a young crew was *Easy Rider,* which appeared in Columbus theaters in October. Produced and directed by thirty-three-year-old Dennis Hopper and twenty-nine-year-old Peter Fonda on a shoestring budget of $400,000, it grossed $60 million, making it one of the most popular movies of the year. *Easy Rider* told the story of a pair of hip characters who motorcycled across America only to meet their ends at the hands of gun-toting rednecks. Coming out six months before the shooting of unarmed students by law enforcement officers at Kent State and Jackson State College in May 1970, it seemed to foreshadow a darker future and has become a cult classic.

Bryce took her parents to see the premiere in November but quickly realized her mistake. Her mother left before the film was over. "Quite simply, *Easy Rider* was too strong for my parents to handle," Bryce wrote. "People like my parents prefer to keep on thinking that things today aren't really that bad.... They worked hard for their security, for their little niche in life, and—after all—they are innocent enough

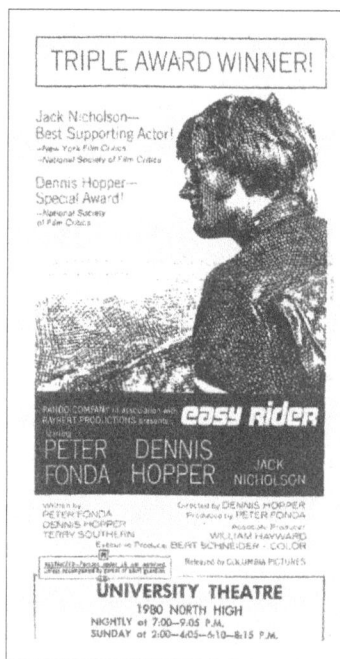

Easy Rider, one of the flood of youth-oriented movies. *Courtesy of the* Lantern.

for much of the wrongdoing. Movies like *Easy Rider* make them worry about too many things."

Another surprise hit of the decade was a three-hour documentary about the 1969 Woodstock music festival. The film appeared in Columbus theaters beginning in July. Bruce Vilanch spotted the film's commercial potential immediately. He said *Woodstock* was an "extraordinary movie… [that was] beautifully put together, never boring, a great commercial re-enactment of a great commercial event, and it's going to make a fortune." And make a fortune it did. After costing only $600,000 to produce, the film grossed $50 million. The best-selling soundtrack album returned even more profit.

PARTY TIME

Centennibrate, Toke Up, and Rock On

After three years of planning and $500,000, officials kicked off Ohio State's one hundredth anniversary on January 10, 1970 in the Ohio Union. The so-called Centennibration event featured entertainment, the crowning of the Centennial Queen, and a three-hundred-pound birthday cake that was designed to serve four thousand people. Other activities continued throughout the spring. Ironically, 1970 would not be remembered for the centennial but for the student protests that closed down the campus between May 7 and May 24.

We Want to Take You Higher

While officials resisted student efforts to legalize 3.2 percent beer in university housing, partygoers found a new diversion. Surveys showed that about one-third of the students admitted to regularly smoking marijuana. Others said they used other drugs, like stimulants and sedatives. Administrators tried to curb drug use by providing educational programs, but students were determined to make their own decisions. Sometimes, that turned out badly. For example, two Smith Hall freshmen found themselves on the wrong side of a fire. The two were away from their room when what was believed to be faulty wiring in an electric guitar burst into flame.

Nine fire trucks responded to the alarm, and the fire was extinguished with no injuries. However, investigators found evidence of drugs and drug paraphernalia in the room and turned the matter over to Columbus police. The students were arrested and charged with possession of narcotics, possession of narcotics instruments and keeping a house where narcotics were kept. The graduate student counselor responsible for the floor told the *Lantern* that the dorm staff was aware that the students were doing drugs and had warned them of the consequences. "We can ask people not to do it, but it's bigger than us," he said.

Soundtrack of the Revolution

More than movies, more than television and more than the written word, music was the soul of the revolutionary 1960s. A shared taste in music bonded the students who came of age in the 1960s unlike any generation before or since. And by the end of the decade, music was changing just like everything else.

The Beatles, who had helped start it all, were breaking up (although the Rolling Stones were still rolling along), Bob Dylan was on the sidelines and Motown was going stale, but newer artists, such as Led Zeppelin, Janis Joplin and Santana, were finding eager audiences for their hard-rock sounds. Meanwhile, the likes of James Taylor, Marvin Gaye and Crosby, Stills, Nash and Young were bringing a softer vibe. Albums became more important than single 45s. The peppy top-forty format at WCOL seemed dated, and more and more people tuned into the new WNCI-FM at 97 to hear progressive rock.

The key to any good party: malt liquor (or other intoxicants), good music and a sound system to blast it at full volume. *Courtesy of the* Lantern.

A party wasn't a party without loud music. A typical stereo package of a turntable, amplifier and bookshelf speakers could easily cost $200 or more (or more than $1,200 in today's prices), but every dorm room, fraternity house and apartment seemed to have at least one stereo blasting out the rhythms of rebellion.

PLACES

Big Changes in the Landscape

The last school year of the decade witnessed the replacement of one High Street landmark with another as well as the continual growth of chain restaurants. However, it did not see an end to parking problems. While it began with an initiative that promised to dramatically change campus life, it failed to do so.

Changes That Didn't Happen

Local tavern owners gathered at Andy Capp's to celebrate the defeat of an effort to make the campus area dry. *From left to right*: Bill Granger of the Varsity Club, Bob Reves of Tenth and High and John Rorris of the Travel Agency (*seated*). *Courtesy of the* Lantern.

A group of university-area residents thought the neighborhood would be a better place to live if the local bars were put out of business. That fall, they succeeded in getting a referendum on the ballot to turn the area dry. Apoplectic bar owners mounted a campaign to oppose the issue. The decision, which affected thousands of students among others, was put up to the 245 voters in those precincts, who had their say on November 4. Votes to keep the campus wet totaled 209, with only 36 "no" votes. Bar supporters heaved a sigh of relief, tipped a big one and continued business as usual.

Changes That Did

In February, the owners of the Cleveland Agora, a popular nightclub in Cleveland, announced they had purchased the State Theater on North High Street with the intention of converting it into what one observer described as a "giant discotheque." The Columbus Agora would include a stage, a large dance floor, a balcony, six bars and room for 1,500 revelers. Admission would be restricted to those with college IDs.

The venue got off to a shaky start. Because promoters were not able to get a certificate of occupancy from the city, students who were at the June 5 opening could listen to two bands for free, but they couldn't dance or drink alcohol. The Agora finally got its act together and became one of the cool places to be in the 1970s. It was renamed the Newport in 1984, and today, it bills itself as "the longest continually running rock club in America."

Another 1970s hotspot, the Oar House, opened in the fall at 1570 North High. In January, Zip Printing opened at 1808 North High Street and in Pearl Alley to provide fast printing. The campus's growing roster of fast-food chains included Burger King at Lane and High and Domino's Pizza, which

The State Theater on High Street became the future site of the Agora, which opened in June 1970. *Courtesy of the* Lantern.

These October 1969 advertisements announced two new businesses that proved to be very popular. *Courtesy of the* Lantern.

offered free delivery from several locations. The influx of fast food took a toll on the area's more traditional restaurants. Margi's, Campus Hi, Hoaky's and Sir Sidneys all closed their doors.

Changing demographics and economics affected other High Street businesses over the years. The blocks south of Eleventh Avenue deteriorated badly before the university stepped in and redeveloped the area through Campus Partners. By 2015, only a handful of establishments from 1970 remained.

Gone to the Dogs

Parking: Worse, Not Better

After endless numbers of consultants, planners, classification schemes and millions of dollars spent on garages, the parking situation at Ohio State was even worse at the end of the decade than when the decade started. While the university increased spaces by 4,550, or 44 percent, permit holders increased by 8,000, or 78 percent. So, instead of having 87 spaces per 100 permits, by the end of the decade, there were only 65 spaces per 100 permits. The traffic jams associated with the opening of classes that fall caused one Columbus patrolman to remark, "I wonder if higher education is really worth all the trouble."

Pooches were a big part of the campus's ambience. After a stray dog bit two students in the spring of 1969, university trustees passed a rule banning unleashed dogs from the Oval. It proved impossible to enforce. *Courtesy of the* Makio.

FASHION

Mini, Midi or Maxi?

Hemlines dominated the fashion buzz in the fall of 1969. Women had a choice of three lengths: mini, midi and maxi. The consensus seemed to be that midis were out, but short skirts with long coats were in. Other trends

Left: Fashion plate 1970: the man boasted pork chop sideburns, a wide belt and watch band and aviator glasses, while his companion sported heavy-duty psychedelic pants. *Courtesy of the* Lantern.

Below: Uniform of the day: although serving in the military grew increasingly unpopular as the Vietnam War dragged on, wearing parts of military uniforms was acceptable. Here, graduating senior Laura Studen (*left*) wore a Vietnam-style jungle jacket as she celebrated her last class at Ohio State. *Courtesy of the* Lantern. The Native American look (*right*) was also popular. *Courtesy of the* Makio.

included aviator sunglasses, the Native American look, the military surplus look and the Afro look, and the question of going braless (or not) was also prevalent. The *Lantern* covered the latter controversy but overcame its usual tendency to appeal to prurient interests by not doing a photo essay. The article concluded that Ohio State women were divided on the matter. Meanwhile, there were plenty of photos of everything else.

BUCKEYE BITS

A New Day

By the spring of 1971, peace had returned to the Oval, but Ohio State was a different place. It had begun moving toward an environment that was more diverse, more open to different points of view, more engaged with the community and more invested in student success. *Courtesy of the* Makio

NOTE ON SOURCES

U nless otherwise indicated, the material for this volume comes from Ohio State's student newspaper, the *Lantern*, or the yearbook, the *Makio*. Back issues of both have been digitized and are available online. The *Lantern* can be found at www.digital.olivesoftware.com/Olive/APA/Ohio. The *Makio* can be found at www.edu.arcasearch.com/usohosy. The student humor magazine, the *Sundial*, has not been digitized, but hard copies are available at University Archives at 2700 Kenny Road in Columbus, Ohio.

The following books also address Ohio State student life in the 1960s, at least in part. William J. Shkurti's *The Ohio State University in the Sixties: The Unraveling of the Old Order* was published by the Ohio State University Press in 2016. Emily Foster's *The Ohio State University District* was published by The History Press in 2014. Raimund Goerler's *The Ohio State University: An Illustrated History* was published by the University Press in 2011. Doreen Uhas Sauer and Stuart Koblentz coauthored *Ohio State University Neighborhoods*, which was published by Arcadia Publishing in 2009.

Several websites contain information on various aspects of student life at Ohio State in the 1960s. These include:

- OSU Archives: www.library.osu.edu/archives
- Larry's Bar: www.larrysbar.com
- WCOL radio: www.columbusmusichistory.com
- BBF restaurant: www.columbusrestaurants.com
- Campus bands: www.buckeyebeat.com

DVDs of Ohio State's 1968 national championship game are available at the university's athletics online store. And for those who can stand it, a video of the Buckeyes' disappointing 1969 loss to Michigan can be found on YouTube.

A number of people contributed to the preparation of this volume. I would like to express appreciation for Tamar Chute and her staff at the OSU Archives, especially reference archivist Michelle Drobik, who put forth a great deal of effort to locate and reproduce the images that were used in this volume. I'd also like thank my colleagues Lynn Bonenberger, Mary Webster and Steve Stover for their editorial assistance and my editors at The History Press, John Rodrigue and Ashley Hill, who tirelessly helped me navigate the challenges of publishing and producing this book. Any errors of omission or commission are the responsibility of the author.

ABOUT THE AUTHOR

ill Shkurti was born and raised in Akron, Ohio, and enrolled at Ohio State University in 1964. He graduated in 1968 with a BA in economics. After serving in the army, Bill returned to Ohio State and earned a master's degree in 1974. He then served in numerous positions for the State of Ohio before he returned to Ohio State as the university's chief financial officer. He retired in 2010 but remains an adjunct professor in the John Glenn College of Public Affairs. He has written extensively about OSU in the 1960s, including a general history titled *Ohio State University in the Sixties: The Unraveling of the Old Order*, which was published by OSU Press in 2016. He and his wife, Renee, who is also an OSU graduate, currently live in Upper Arlington.

Visit us at
www.historypress.com